NEW LONDON STYLE

NEW LONDON STYLE

CHLOE GRIMSHAW
PHOTOGRAPHS BY INGRID RASMUSSEN

with 371 illustrations, 350 in colour

Thames & Hudson

First published in the United Kingdom in 2008 by
Thames & Hudson Ltd, 181A High Holborn,
London WC1V 7QX

www.thamesandhudson.com

First paperback edition 2010

Reprinted 2010

British Library Cataloguing-in-Publication Data
A catalogue record for this book is available from the British Library

ISBN 978-0-500-28847-4

Design: SMITH
Victoria Forrest, Lesley Gilmour
www.smith-design.com

Printed and bound in Singapore by Tien Wah Press (Pte) Ltd

When my grandfather, the art critic John Russell, wrote about London for Thames & Hudson in 1994, we all took a moment to reconsider the city. Through his approach, questioning how and why we live in a city, I wanted to explore how much London has changed over the past fourteen years.

Creating *New London Style* would have been impossible without the patience and generosity of its residents, many of whom have revealed their design secrets and favourite vintage stores. Thank you to everyone who invited us into their homes and encouraged us with endless cups of tea and coffee! We feel privileged to have been the first to photograph the homes of Carole Conrad, Jane Collins, Nikki Tibbles, Matthew Williamson and Erin O'Connor for our book, and are very grateful to have had this opportunity.

It was fascinating to learn more about the history of London, from Norman Ackroyd's guide to Bermondsey, to Langlands + Bell's description of Whitechapel, and finally Sam Robinson's invaluable guide to Notting Hill's most stylish homeowners and favourite antique shops. Only London's residents know every aspect of their streets in detail and the history of their neighbourhood; it has been a wonderful experience for us to learn more about each corner of the city.

Thanks also to the great team at Thames & Hudson, it was fantastic to work with Elain McAlpine, Sadie Butler and Lucas Dietrich again.

Chloe Grimshaw + Ingrid Rasmussen
London, 2008

Previous page: In Adam Hills and Maria Speake's Marylebone penthouse flat, fabric designed by Adam's architect father in the 1970s provides a striking contrast to the cityscape beyond.

NEW LONDON STYLE

NW1, NW3, NW6 **Primrose Hill, Hampstead, Brondesbury + Queen's Park**
- **Victoria Marriott + Craig Matson** Architects/owners of Roundhouse Design
- **Matthew Williamson** Fashion designer
- **Jo Berryman** Fashion stylist
- **Harvey Bertram-Brown** Art director
- **Gillian Anderson-Price** Owner of Judith Michael & Daughter boutique
- **Martha Krempel** Furniture designer
- **Bill Amberg + Susie Forbes** Leather designer and magazine editor

SE1, SE5, SE22, SW3, SW6, SW7, SW9 **Bermondsey, Camberwell, East Dulwich, Chelsea, Parson's Green, South Kensington + Brixton**
- **Norman Ackroyd** Artist
- **Peggy Prendeville** Artist and interior designer
- **Erin O'Connor** Fashion model
- **Rob + Josie da Bank** Radio 1 DJ and organizers of Bestival
- **Tracey Boyd** Fashion designer
- **Annabel Dearlove** Parson's Green homeowner
- **Annabel Lewis** Owner of V.V. Rouleaux haberdashery
- **Tobit Roche + Nancy Oakley** Artist and fashion PR director

E1, E9, EC1, EC2 **Whitechapel, Hackney, Clerkenwell + Shoreditch**
- **Les Trois Garçons** Interior designers and restaurateurs
- **Langlands + Bell** Artists
- **Lisa Whatmough** Furniture designer
- **Daisy de Villeneuve** Artist and illustrator
- **Emily Chalmers** Interiors stylist

W1, W2, W8, W10, W11 **Marylebone, Bayswater, Kensington, North Kensington + Notting Hill**
- **Adam Hills + Maria Speake** Owners of salvage firm Retrouvius
- **Jane Collins** Owner of Sixty6 boutique
- **Simon Templeton** Architect
- **Carole Conrad** Patron of the arts
- **Justin Thornton + Thea Bregazzi** Fashion designers
- **Sam Robinson** Owner of The Cross boutique
- **Carina Cooper** Food writer
- **Nikki Tibbles** Owner of Wild at Heart florists

INTRODUCTION

The unique and quirky sense of style that is now firmly associated with London is reflected in the homes of its residents. Many of the artists, stylists and designers featured within these pages have customized furniture and textiles and built up art collections over the decades to echo their individual passions and personalities. Creating these spaces is a labour of love – it takes years of looking, dreaming and collecting before a house truly becomes a home.

The unifying factor of the New London Style is this desire to create something original, rather than slavishly following the latest trends. Inspired to create one-off designs of their own, two homeowners, Simon Templeton (p. 180) and Carole Conrad (p. 186), each commissioned custom-built staircases; Simon for his Bayswater mews house, and Carole for her architect-designed penthouse flat in one of the world's most exclusive streets. Stylist Emily Chalmers (p. 156), though working within a more limited budget, was equally single-minded, and scoured markets and charity shops for the perfect pieces for her open-plan Shoreditch warehouse. Vintage furniture, from the strong shapes of the Victorian period to the clean lines of twentieth-century design, can create a personal and individual look, and salvage pieces, too, can contribute to the unique feel of a space. In their Marylebone flat, Adam Hills and Maria Speake (p. 168) transformed marble counters from a former fishmonger's into kitchen counters, while in Parson's Green discarded silkscreens from a wallpaper factory became artwork for Annabel Dearlove's bedroom (p. 106).

Just as London girls shun the head-to-toe designer look, preferring instead to pair a Primark dress with a Marni handbag, the same approach applies to their homes. Artist Daisy de Villeneuve (p. 150) has draped a dress from Missoni over the cupboard door in her Clerkenwell flat, while florist Nikki Tibbles (p. 214) hunts out quirky vases at Kempton Antiques Market for her home in Notting Hill. And when fashion designer Matthew Williamson (p. 22) couldn't find the right furniture for his Hampstead cottage, he asked design firm Tann-Rokka to create bespoke pieces. Working with an interior designer can often push homeowners to experiment with their own style; for model Erin O'Connor (p. 84), it was a revelation to collaborate with stylist Suzy Hoodless, who encouraged her client to mix vintage Chesterfield sofas with such playful elements as teacup-print wallpaper.

In every area of London, synagogues, pubs, churches and schools are being imaginatively converted into stylish living accommodation. Petrol stations have been torn down and replaced with luxury flats, and old garages and stables converted into stylish mews houses. The three artistic minds behind Les Trois Garçons (p. 130) live in a listed building in Whitechapel that was originally a Victorian pub, nicknamed 'The Birdhouse' because of the bird traders who would gather here with their wares. Living in a unique building also created a new set of challenges for both artist Norman Ackroyd (p. 68), with his eighteenth-century Bermondsey warehouse, and interior designer Peggy Prendeville (p. 76), with her converted Edwardian chapel in Camberwell. By collecting vintage plan chests and printing tables, Norman has kept close to the building's industrial past, whereas Peggy wanted to steer clear of too many ecclesiastical references and commissioned contemporary pieces as a response to the extraordinary marble floor and fleur-de-lis decoration of the former chapel.

Property in London is now among the most expensive in the world, and aspiring homeowners have to be determined and resourceful in finding somewhere to live. Londoners use every inch of available space: turning the loft into an extra bedroom, extending the house into the garden, or excavating the basement to create another room. Despite its rocketing property prices, London has always been defined by a certain individuality. The city is recognized around the world for its creative industries – such as music, fashion, design and architecture – and its homes reflect this free-spirited approach, where personal style is prized above expensive accessories or designer kitchens. Where else could you find an Underground map recycled as a dining table, or a bench from a chemical laboratory turned into kitchen units? The New London Style can only be defined by the design aesthetic – sometimes eccentric, always inspiring – of its residents.

NW1, NW3, NW6
PRIMROSE HILL
HAMPSTEAD
BRONDESBURY
QUEEN'S PARK

Primrose Hill has been home to London's literary élite throughout the modern era, with Karl Marx, W.B. Yeats, Sylvia Plath and Kingsley Amis all making their homes here. The neighbourhood's focal point is Primrose Hill park, which reaches over 78 metres at its highest point and affords panoramic views across London to Canary Wharf and the Millennium Dome in the east and to the chimneys of Battersea Power Station in the west. Enclosed by the Crown in 1842, the area's landmark Victorian squares and crescents were built up around the newly public park throughout the nineteenth century.

Just north of Primrose Hill is Hampstead, one of the most expensive places to live in London, with more millionaires living here than in any other part of the city. Traditionally known as an artistic and literary enclave from the eighteenth century onwards, Hampstead still has an intellectual reputation. It is the highest point in London, and then as now was considered the perfect place to get away from it all. Although Dickens wrote about gritty London life, he preferred to live in Hampstead's rural open spaces. Keats was inspired by his evening walks here to write 'Ode to a Nightingale', and Constable painted views from the heath before returning to his home in nearby Well Walk.

Brondesbury, too, was primarily rural before its railway station opened in 1860. Thereafter it became a desirable residential area, with large Victorian villas built along its tree-lined streets. Nearby Queen's Park came into being after Queen Victoria opened the Royal Agricultural Society show here in 1879, and a permanent site of thirty acres was later developed. Over two thousand homes were built in a distinctive Gothic-revival style between 1870 and 1890. This family-friendly neighbourhood is now home to actress Thandie Newton, *Vogue* editor Alexandra Shulman and rock-chick-turned-designer Jade Jagger.

VICTORIA MARRIOTT + CRAIG MATSON
PRIMROSE HILL

This Victorian terraced house in a leafy neighbourhood of northwest London has been home to three generations of one stylish, design-orientated family.

Three generations of the Marriott family have lived in Primrose Hill since the 1950s: the architect Philip Marriott bought the Victorian terraced house here in 1958; his daughters Victoria and Sophia inherited the house in the late 1980s and lived here together with their families for over a decade; and now Victoria lives here with her architect partner Craig Matson and their young family. Victoria and Craig, who set up contemporary design firm Roundhouse in 1996 to create bespoke kitchens, storage and furniture, bought out Sophia's share of the house in 2002 and set about redesigning it, using the most innovative Roundhouse techniques to create a comfortable and stylish family home.

When Victoria and Sophia were renovating the house themselves, their first step was to restore the plaster cornicing. 'We used to stand on a ladder with a steamer, and pick all of the old paint out of the plaster,' remembers Victoria. 'The whole process took weeks.' When some of the cornicing came loose, the sisters had new pieces made up to match at Butcher Plasterworks, just around the corner. Rather than paint it again, the sisters chose to leave the cornicing in its natural state, as they were worried about losing some of the intricate detail that they had so painstakingly revealed. Walls and ceilings were also stripped back, as the girls loved the patina of the old plaster. They even found some old drawings and diagrams drawn onto the wall by their father years ago as he was working out designs for bedrooms and a wardrobe.

Having grown up in the house as a child, a sense of family is incredibly important to Victoria, and she loves having the big L-shaped sofa in the sitting room that everyone can pile onto. Mementoes are displayed on shelves around the room, such as fossils and twigs from her family's house in Dorset, as is a glass bottle filled with sand from Cottesloe beach in Australia, where Craig grew up, and a perforated steel pinboard made by Victoria is home to a display of family drawings and photographs. It's the contrast between old and new that gives this house its character, and Victoria and Craig have taken full advantage of the opportunity to experiment with materials and textures. Within the kitchen, a stainless-steel worktop and glossy white cabinets contrast with pink neon up-lighting. A long, low wooden bench separates the kitchen from the dining area, and also doubles up as a useful storage area for kitchen crockery. The dining table extends out from the wall, and can easily seat up to ten people. 'It's not so much that we love cooking,' explains Victoria. 'It's more that if Sophia and [brother-in-law] Richard come round with the kids, then there's already nine of us. We used to have to do it in shifts, with the children eating first, but now we can all fit round the table.' The narrow galley kitchen initially appears to be quite a small space, but with the folding glass doors opened out onto the garden, it feels more like an outdoor room. Having porcelain tiles on the kitchen floor that extend out into the garden helps to enhance this feeling of spaciousness.

The couple decided to put all of the living spaces on the ground floor, leaving them with a generous amount of space on the first floor out of which to create bookshelves and a study, along with a compact bathroom and large bedroom. Victoria chose to mix family heirloom pieces, including her grandmother's chairs and her parents' mirror, with the more contemporary pieces that she has designed with Craig. They both enjoyed thinking about every inch of space and considering every detail, such as how much storage they would need and how to light the bedroom. All of the furniture and shelving was custom-built to fit each alcove and each particular length of wall. Speaking as a true designer, Victoria admits that 'the way the room felt and how the wardrobe fitted in the room were more important that trying to accommodate all of my clothes.'

The second floor of the house has been given over to the couple's two daughters, Lily and Dora, who have their own kitchenette and bathroom, along with a den/chill-out space in the attic. For the time being, they seem to prefer spending time with their parents downstairs, but Victoria admits that this may soon change. Lily's room has been stylishly furnished with an antique mirror and vintage-style wallpaper, so it may not be too long before she, too, follows in the footsteps of her design-led family.

The vintage signs for Brymay Redheads matches are from Craig's hometown of Margaret River, Australia, and are displayed against the distressed plaster walls of the hallway.

Craig's love of gadgets can be seen in the Meccano Eiffel tower (put together on the Eurostar back from Paris!), while the large gold 'M' is a Marriott family heirloom and used to hang on the back of the front door. The sitting room has a 1960s feel with its Modernist black leather Cassina sofa from Chaplins and '60s-inspired lamp from Heal's. The deep-brown floorboards are made from fired oak.

The large dining table and the low wooden bench were both designed by the couple; additional seating is supplied by the Arne Jacobsen-inspired chairs. Overhead is a 1930s chandelier from Rainbow.

Displayed prominently on a shelf are pieces by local potter Fliff Lidsey, including a swirly plate and cup and saucer, while a pair of teddy bears and Stella Vic the cat find a cosy spot on Victoria's bed.

Decades of use and collecting have given the house a comfortable, lived-in feel. The wooden chair belonged to Victoria's grandmother, and the staircase that Victoria is seen climbing is original to the mid-nineteenth-century building, with its steps polished smooth by generations of homeowners. The stripped-back plaster and cornicing look whimsical and elegant when set off by a vintage chandelier.

NW3

MATTHEW WILLIAMSON
HAMPSTEAD

In this cottage in Hampstead, bright colours and flamboyant touches are just what one would expect from this world-renowned fashion designer.

Matthew Williamson, a revered name in the world of fashion, celebrated ten years in the industry with a retrospective exhibition at London's Design Museum in 2007. Clients such as model-turned-photographer Helena Christensen, actress Sienna Miller and designer Jade Jagger flock to his ornate Mayfair boutique, decorated with hand-painted wallpaper, to pick out designs in his bright prints and bold colours. Matthew's work commitments as the creative director for Pucci as well as a highly successful designer in his own right means that he divides his time equally between Florence and London. To take time out from his busy schedule and to find the peace and quiet he craves, Matthew recently decided to buy a cottage overlooking Hampstead Heath. It's as close to country living as you are ever going to find in a capital city: 'Living here energizes and inspires me,' Matthew explains. 'I like living close to nature, and I love the village atmosphere.'

Matthew's signature style draws on his passion for embroidery and textiles, and he wanted his home to reflect his love of colour and print. He likes to contrast modern design and clean lines with embellished decoration and vivid colours, a preference Matthew shares with the designers at interiors firm Tann-Rokka, who are friends of long standing. This shared vision led to the creation of such items as the mirrored armchair and the electric blue sofa in the sitting room specifically for the cottage. These contemporary pieces contrast with an embroidered boho-chic sofa, which is piled high with bespoke cushions, fashioned from the armfuls of textiles and saris that Matthew returned home with after his inspirational travels to Morocco, Italy and India.

Rather than getting too hung up on hippy-chic design, Matthew also likes to collect key Modernist pieces for his home, such as the marble Eero Saarinen dining table and bright-green dining chairs by Charles and Ray Eames. The flooring throughout the open-plan ground-floor space is white rubber from Dalsouple, chosen to act as a foil to the bright array of colours, including the bright-green walls and pink fluorescent lighting of the kitchen. Above the dining table is a chandelier, painted with a white gloss paint, which looks as if it is about to drip onto the table – a witty piece of contemporary design from Mint. The green contemporary side-table reflects Matthew's eclectic taste, with its huge rococo gilt mirror, an array of blue and yellow glass vases from the 1960s, and a vintage glass clown.

A soft black carpet leads upstairs to the bedroom, and is illuminated by a neon sculpture, which slowly transforms into hundreds of different shades. On the facing wall is a set of antlers above favourite photographs of models, actors and friends wearing Matthew's designs. As if to underline the fact that his work is not just about hippy vibes, Matthew chose an intricate monochrome wallpaper for his bedroom by up-and-coming designers Rodnik; on closer inspection, the 'flower' pattern turns out to be a macabre design of ribs and spinal cords. Against the wallpaper is a 1960s-style chair, the result of Matthew's recent collaboration with Capellini and Pucci. And just to show that he is not obsessed with designer labels for the home, his bedspread is from Habitat (albeit from his own collection) and the glass bedside lamps are from John Lewis.

Matthew lives a life of extremes, constantly travelling from Italy to India, and back to London via Morocco. His home has become a real sanctuary, a place to close the door on work and to relax with good friends. He admits that although he is not a very good cook, he is a great host, mixing cocktails and entertaining guests until the early hours. Matthew's flamboyant style, incorporating splashes of hot pink, decorative wallpaper and carefully chosen design classics, can be seen in every room of this rural retreat in North London.

Having been a fan of Rob and Nick Carter's neon artworks for many years, Matthew wanted to illuminate his home with a glowing rainbow light that works equally well as a piece of modern sculpture.

White rubber flooring contrasts with mirrored tiles from **Intertiles** and fluorescent paint trim on the window, while an electric-blue sofa from **Tann-Rokka** is a dramatic foil to the black-and-white teapot and cup and saucer from **Mint**. In the bedroom, a Pucci chair sits comfortably with a bedspread from Matthew's collection for **Habitat** (covering a bed from **Liberty**) and unusually patterned wallpaper from **Rodnik**.

Favourite objects are displayed against the bright-green walls of the kitchen, including this cheerful pink Buddha lamp from lighting specialist Shiu-Kay Kan. Matthew's small courtyard garden was designed to have a Mediterranean feel, complete with orange and lemon trees. The white-painted chair from Petersham Nurseries was reupholstered by Matthew's mum Maureen in fabric from Pucci.

A patterned sofa from **Liberty** is home to a bevy of brightly coloured cushions. In the dining room, a green table is topped by a gold mirror from **Tann-Rokka** and glass vases from **Absolute Flowers**, while an Eero Saarinen dining table and Eames chairs are accented by a witty 'dripping' chandelier from **Mint**. The black-painted walls and black carpet contrast with the vivid colours and patterns of the bedroom.

JO BERRYMAN
HAMPSTEAD

Rock-'n'-roll meets high fashion in this Edwardian brick house in Hampstead, where the sophisticated boudoir-chic feel is tempered by cheekily humorous touches.

Keen to put down roots in leafy Hampstead, fashion stylist Jo Berryman searched the area for a family home before coming across this large, red-brick Edwardian house in the spring of 2005. The magnolia tree in the front garden was in full bloom, and the double-fronted building was flooded with light. 'It had a wonderful feeling,' remembers Jo. 'As soon as I walked through the door, I knew that it could be a lovely home.' The house needed six months of structural work, but once it was complete, Jo combed antiques markets and architectural salvage yards to come up with a unique look that was all her own.

To create an entertaining space on the ground floor for friends and family, Jo chose to build a kitchen-cum-dining room to one side of the sweeping wooden staircase, which leads out into the garden, and a living area on the other, which stretches back along the entire length of the house. The sleek design and industrial chic of the Boffi kitchen makes a great contrast to the more nostalgic, vintage feel to the rest of the home. Steps lead down into the intimate dining room, which is set beneath a skylight, with windows overlooking the garden. The sitting room is filled with antiques and junk-shop finds, including a circular sofa from the 1970s and a round, acid-etched pewter table from Alfies Antique Market, which is decorated in silvery greys and burgundy to contrast with the pink prettiness of the magnolia tree outside. Jo loves textiles and contrasting patterns, and chose two colourways of the same wallpaper pattern from Cole & Son to divide the room into two distinct areas. At the rear of the room, overlooking the garden, is a white baby grand piano, set atop a 'Squiggle' print rug by Vivienne Westwood. The walls are papered with a pale blue paisley design and offset by antique white-lacquered Chinese cabinets with inlaid mirrors, together with large blue jars designed by Jo's friend, Mags.

Jo converted the entire first floor into one large area comprising bedroom, dressing room, walk-in wardrobe and bathroom. Inspired by stylish hotel rooms, she wanted this space to exude indulgence. Jo ordered a 'handsome-looking' Savoir No. 2 bed (originally designed for the Savoy Hotel in London's Strand) in order to 'channel that old-style Hollywood glamour, with a bit of Château Marmont thrown in.' When decorating the space, Jo imagined 'a Hollywood starlet wafting about on a zebra rug and wearing a Champagne-coloured negligée,' and to complement this glamorous 1930s and '40s feel, she chose delicate shagreen bedside tables and Art Déco lamps with fringed shades. Rather than have a real zebra-skin rug, she chose instead a chic Diane von Furstenberg design for The Rug Company. On the walls hang a small collection of nudes, ranging from an oil by David Cobley (whose work can be seen in the National Portrait Gallery) to a vintage painting from Fandango in Islington. One of Jo's favourite pieces is the gold lettering reading 'Love Me' by New York City-based graffiti artist Julia Change. At the opposite end of the room is the dressing area, with a pewter bateau bath set beneath the window. Next to the bath, Jo placed a carved, baroque wooden table, a family heirloom that 'looks so Masonic, but could also be Indian.' It is an eclectic piece with a carved wooden egg suspended between the table legs. Jo has a bath every night before bed without fail, and loves to have this time alone to meditate and reflect on her day. The bathroom is a much more functional space, with lots of marble and mirrors, very much inspired by the luxurious Mercer Hotel in New York's SoHo. There is a long marble sink and a marble shower room with benches at each end, which doubles up as a hammam.

On the second-floor is an intimate snug with amazing views over the Hampstead treetops and the London skyline. This is the one area where DVDs and CDs are allowed in the house, as Jo prefers not to have too many televisions or stereos about the place. There is a humorous British vibe to this room with cheeky references to the Union Jack, from a 'Jubilee' needlepoint tapestry by Lucinda Chambers on the wall to a Vivienne Westwood tobacco-stained cushion, both for The Rug Company. Renovating and decorating the house gave Jo a new-found appreciation for interior design. She loved all of the different elements, from picking out the smoky-grey wooden floors to choosing the Colefax & Fowler curtains and the vintage furniture. She is even thinking of embarking on a new career as an interior designer, but for the time being is thrilled to have created such a quirky, vintage-inspired home.

A carved rabbit perches atop a pile of art and design books, set against a backdrop of 'Mimosa' wallpaper from Cole & Son.

The vintage desk and chair, seen here in Jo's study, are from architectural salvage firm **Retrouvius**, while the staircase in the hallway is original to the Edwardian house, as are the smoky-grey floorboards. In the sitting room, the bold **Damien Hirst** print above the mantelpiece provides a striking contrast to the feather-print **Cole & Son** wallpaper and vintage rose-patterned fireguard.

Jo created a boudoir feel in the combination bathroom/dressing room with a vibrant **Osborne & Little** print for the curtains, an African-inspired rug by **Diane Von Furstenberg** for **The Rug Company**, and shapely chairs from **George Smith**. In the bedroom, she added shagreen bedside tables from the 1970s for a more masculine feel; their bold, modern design complements the simple **Art Déco** lamps.

Jo loves the humorous British vibe of the snug, with its Chesterfield sofa – given a modern twist via velvet upholstery – and Union Jack theme. The 'Jubilee' needlepoint on the wall is by Lucinda Chambers for The Rug Company. Quirky vintage finds, such as this kitsch Yorkie painting and rococo-inspired chair from Alfies Antique Market, have pride of place, together with a collection of platinum discs.

HARVEY BERTRAM-BROWN
HAMPSTEAD

The need for a fresh start and a new home led one art director to create this funky, high-design pad in Hampstead.

For designer Harvey Bertram-Brown, creating dramatic interiors is second nature. Together he and business partner Carolyn Corbett (who met while students at the Royal College of Art) run design company The New Renaissance, and their work ranges from decorating store windows for über-luxe department store Harvey Nichols to styling Boy George and directing videos for Elton John. When it came to designing his own home, however, Harvey wanted to create a cool, white sanctuary, somewhere to retreat to from the rigours of his hectic work schedule.

Following the recent break-up of a relationship, Harvey was ready for a fresh start and wanted to move into a house, rather than a flat. As he recalls, 'I wanted to have my own front door, so that I could create an atmosphere, as soon as you walk in.' He needed enough space for a guest-room, a children's room (for his seven nephews and nieces!) and a large study. Looking for his new home nearly became a full-time job, as Harvey would drive around Hampstead every day looking for new properties, as well as searching the Internet and working with eight different estate agents. It took four months and over a hundred properties before Harvey found his ideal house, which had been empty for over a year. 'It was a tiny little rabbit warren filled with really small rooms,' remembers Harvey, 'and it smelled of drains.' No one else was convinced by the property, but Harvey could see its potential.

Harvey decided early on that his new house would be predominantly white, and he worked with a specialist company to install floor-to-ceiling white rubber (more commonly used as surfaces for science labs) throughout the house, even in the bathrooms. Inspired by London's Sanderson Hotel, Harvey initially wanted to install similar net curtains, but eventually found some white-fringed ones in Habitat for a fraction of the cost, which he cut to fit the windows. The only room that breaks with this colour scheme is the intimate sitting room, which is decorated in a palette of chocolate brown, lilac and white. Harvey's love of reflective surfaces and mirrors led to the acquisition of a chrome lamp from Tom Dixon and a mirrored bird from Aria. This small room is all about texture, from the cowhide rug and suede sofa to the polished wooden storage units and the lilac-and-silver wallpaper.

Because he regularly invites friends and family over to the house, Harvey wanted to get the design of the kitchen absolutely right and worked with a designer to create a made-to-measure space with granite work surfaces and bright-green splashbacks. Overhead is a vintage light fixture, with a cord that allows it to be hung at any chosen height. Everything is immaculately tidy: 'I get claustrophobic if I have too many things out,' Harvey explains. 'I love that country-kitchen look, but I just can't live like that. My natural aesthetic is clutter, clutter, clutter – but you have to have a bit of space to breathe around you, especially when you have been working really intensely.' His study mixes a romantic style with a more industrial feel: tree-print wallpaper from Cole & Son contrasts with a vintage stainless-steel storage unit and a chandelier made from a cluster of light bulbs, and glass-fronted boxes on the walls display favourite images and document seventeen years of The New Renaissance. It's an elegant solution, and Harvey just feels relieved 'not to have schmuck out on little shelves collecting dust, or photos in albums that are never opened.'

In the bedroom, this hard-edged glamour is combined with a shabby-chic style, where Harvey's desire for 'a really romantic space' is seen in the Louis XIV-inspired bed and armchair, painted white to contrast with glossy black modern fittings including bedside tables, a lacquered cabinet and a chandelier. Inspired by *Sex And The City*, Harvey was keen to create a Carrie Bradshaw-style walk-through wardrobe, as he likes to have everything colour-coordinated and neatly on display. But when it came to decorating the guest bedrooms, Harvey indulged his playful side, choosing bright-pink cushions and a glamorous bathroom for the main guest bedroom and a forest theme – with inspiration from Sylvester the Cat – for the children's room. As he travels so much for work, Harvey always ends up bringing things back for his home, including some fluorescent pink skins from South Africa. Harvey bought the huge 1960s-style television to celebrate working on an Elton John video, while the pink 'Love' cushions in the children's room were props for a video for British pop star Rachel Stevens.

Moving into his new home was about drawing a line beneath one chapter in his life and starting afresh. Harvey sold most of his belongings from his previous flat and just kept the pieces that he really loved: favourite pictures, photographs and a cosy sofa. He has found it an incredibly cathartic experience to create a completely new space and to design a vibrant, modern home.

Harvey's dedication to his work as an art director even extends to creating the most stylish dog kennel in town for his partner's pampered pooch.

The linked mirror was a gift from **B**oy **G**eorge (it used to hang in the singer's **N**ew York home in the 1980s). In the guest bathroom, Harvey created a feel of vintage glamour with reproductions from **B**athstore.

Overleaf: Granite work surfaces in the custom-built kitchen are set off by bespoke splashbacks from **G**lass **D**eco. The ceramics are by Jonathan **A**dler and the 'Bombo' stool is by Stefano **G**iovannoni.

...G of DEPOSITING
...BBISH in this FIELD will b...
...ROSECUTED.   R. LITTLE.
                BANK FOOT.
...ne 1923.   NEWTON REIGNY.

GILLIAN ANDERSON-PRICE
HAMPSTEAD

A second-generation antiques shop owner brings a collector's eye for detail to this Georgian cottage in North London.

When Gillian Anderson-Price moved to Hampstead with her young son Sevy, she was concerned about living in an old-fashioned villagey neighbourhood 'with not enough young vibes'. But after walking around the block with Sevy in his pram, she was completely won over by the bakery, flower shop and traditional tearooms that she found just steps from her door. Keen to follow in her mother's footsteps (mum Judith ran Judith Michael Antiques in Corbridge, Northumberland), Gillian opened her own vintage store, Judith Michael & Daughter, on Hampstead's Haverstock Hill in 2002, before relocating to Primrose Hill in 2005. Now that her mother's shop has closed, Gillian's intimate boutique acts as a reflection of her own taste and interests, which range from vintage books, prints and magazines to elegant mirrors, antique scent bottles and candlesticks.

Gillian's Georgian cottage had belonged to the Shepherd family since the eighteenth century, and still retained plenty of its original features. It would originally have been used as a staff cottage for the main house, but Gillian has another name for it: 'I call it the doll's house, because it is so tiny!' The layout of the house felt dated, with four bedrooms upstairs and a bathroom on the ground floor behind the kitchen, so she turned one of the upstairs bedrooms into a bathroom. 'I didn't think you needed four bedrooms in such a little house,' Gillian recalls laughingly. To create more space and bring in more light to her petite cottage, she built an extension out into the garden for the kitchen and conservatory, but was left with 'a tiny postage-stamp garden'. On reflection, she feels that it was worth making the changes because 'the space we've gained indoors is more useful than the outside space we lost.'

With such a huge collection of antiques in storage, Gillian had almost too much furniture to choose from. Luckily, the house itself helped her to make a decision, as the narrow staircase prohibited any furniture apart from the flat-pack variety and the smallest objects from being carried upstairs. On the ground floor, Gillian was able to indulge her taste a little more, with a grand dining table and candelabra placed beneath a painting on stainless steel by Rory Dobner. Most of the portraits in oils belonged to Gillian's grandmother, and she particularly likes the one of a young boy above the sofa. The sitting room is a contrast between very modern and very old, with pieces from the eighteenth century and the Victorian period jostling for space with those from the 1930s and the twenty-first century.

To soften the look of the stark black-and-white bathroom, with its crisp white tiles and slate floor, Gillian put up a black lace curtain and decided to display her collection of ebony Victorian hand mirrors (she has nearly thirty!) as a graphic statement against the white walls. If it had been up to her, she would have covered a whole wall with mirrors, but was inspired by a friend to hang them at eye level in a straight line for more impact. 'I've always thought a collection of anything looks fantastic,' she says. 'I don't think it matters what you collect. With the right display, it can look amazing.' She admits that she went a bit crazy for flags in Sevy's room, collecting vintage bunting to hang on the walls and Union Jack print to turn into cushions and a bedspread, against which a vintage Steiff teddy reclines. For her own attic bedroom, Gillian wanted to create the feel of a secret hideaway and hung tree-print wallpaper from Cole & Son on the sloping walls and a huge swathe of taffeta curtains from Zoffany over the window. Her favourite pieces of furniture, such as the antique bateau-lit bed and the French wardrobe, were all taken apart and carried upstairs. Gillian flung a vintage satin shawl over an antique armchair and displayed candles and delicate handbags to add to the romantic feel. Rather than take a more obvious route and collect antique crucifixes, Gillian was instead drawn to the orbs and crowns originally made for French churches. Part of this new collection is now displayed on her bedside table, beneath a favourite wooden sign.

Buying and selling for the shop means that Gillian is out the door by 4am at least once a week. She has to remind herself not to take the best things home, and saves her favourite pieces for the shop. Only the most eclectic or undistinguished pieces end up in her home, but somehow Gillian can display them to look like treasured antiques. Even Sevy is starting to take an interest in the family business, and has just brought home his first object from the shop: a Victorian toucan in a glass case, complete with painted beetles. Despite settling into family life in Hampstead, there is no chance of Gillian and Sevy conforming to a conventional lifestyle any time soon.

A crown-topped orb from a French church is displayed on Gillian's bedside table, against wallpaper in 'Woods' from Cole & Son.

Paintings from the shop are mixed in with family heirlooms, and are displayed above the wooden staircase leading to the bedrooms. One corner of Gillian's bedroom has been turned into a dressing room, with the original eighteenth-century cupboard and antique luggage used for storage. In the sitting room, vintage luggage also doubles up as a side-table. The portrait in oils belonged to Gillian's grandmother.

The bathroom has a graphic black-and-white feel, complemented by Gillian's collection of Victorian hand mirrors. In Sevy's bedroom, the Union Jack appears on bunting, bedlinen, and even on an old needlepoint hung above the bed. The walls of the downstairs cloakroom are papered with a red paisley design, while the door doubles up as space for vintage handbags and stylish wraps.

The dining room reveals how Gillian mixes it up by placing antique and contemporary pieces side by side: the painting on stainless steel by Rory Dobner sits comfortably with Victorian furniture and a silver candelabra. In the light-filled, glass-topped conservatory, artworks are regularly changed around and vary from a portrait of the young Elizabeth II to anatomical diagrams, both propped against the walls.

MARTHA KREMPEL
BRONDESBURY

A quiet corner in northwest London provides the perfect setting for a Victorian villa belonging to an interiors designer and her family.

When Martha Krempel was a student at art college in the late 1980s, she specialized in huge structures made out of cement and metal. This early love of three-dimensional, large-scale work eventually translated into a passion for furniture design and interiors. One of her first projects on leaving college was to design the Big Sky photographic studio, in Islington, based on the work of Mexican architect Luis Barragán. 'We divided things up with big blocks of colour, with a narrow gap in between, to give a vista,' Martha recalls. She sold her share in the company and started a new business with designer Tanya Thompson making lighting and furniture, before going on to set up her own interior design firm. Contrasting commercial projects with designing houses, Martha explains that 'with houses, it's much more personal. There is a lot of empathy going on, and even a bit of counselling.'

Martha and the rest of the family moved into their own Brondesbury house, a large Victorian villa, during the eclipse of 2000. The house had a large garden, edged with mature trees, a real bonus as far as the family was concerned: 'There's something blissful about having privacy in London,' Martha states. Fortunately, the building itself was structurally sound, which left Martha free to focus on the design of the interiors. 'When we first moved in here, we only had three items of furniture in our possession,' she remembers, 'a white armoire, a white-painted metal bed, and a table.' She recalls, too – with some dismay – that her seven-month-old daughter had nothing to pull herself up on to help her learn to walk. Martha chose to concentrate on colour and texture, mixing Marimekko prints, vintage fabric and sheepskin rugs to create a warm, vibrant feel. If she can't find an artwork that produces the exact effect that she wants, she heads to Marimekko or Maisonette for fabric to stretch over wooden frames to her own specification. Above the sitting-room fireplace is a delicate photograph of a forest by Nigel Shafran (if you look closely, you can see a bird's nest in the branches), its fragility echoed by Martha's collection of glass candlesticks, displayed on the mantelpiece. Splashes of colour in the hallway are provided with a bench cushion, also from Marimekko, and one of Martha's own canvases, placed between two hand-blown lamps.

The study at the back of the house, overlooking the garden, made the perfect place for Martha's studio. She works from a 1950s Danish rosewood desk, which has a lamp made to her own design, with a shade fashioned from Cole & Son wallpaper in 'Woods'. Found objects and favourite artworks are displayed on the wall above a Chesterfield sofa bought at auction, with her own bikini print placed next to a piece by Peter Saville and an animal skull found in Mexico. When Martha buys contemporary design, she prefers to mix it up with vintage pieces: in the sitting room, B&B Italia sofas – piled high with cushions designed by Tanya Thompson for Made – are placed next to a 1950s-style chair, for example, while an old wooden coffee table works well against a contemporary rug from The Rug Company. In the snug, Martha has hung framed photographs of her children to create an asymmetric display. She picked up the 1960s-style lamp from Mint, and the armchair, accented with cushions from The Conran Shop and The Cross, is a classic design from George Smith. Martha's personal style can be seen in the bedroom, which features pieces by creative friends, such as Tanya's huge sheepskin rug and Nikki Tibbles' quilts and throws (for Nikki's own house, see p. 214). Her collection of contemporary and antique vases is displayed on the chest-of-drawers and bedside tables, next to favourite artworks. She couldn't resist customizing certain pieces, stretching some print fabric from Liberty to create a canvas in the bathroom, and painting a vintage chair from the 1950s in peony pink to liven up the bedroom.

Very few designers ever feel that their home is totally finished, and Martha is no exception. She is already planning how to redesign the ground floor, moving the kitchen to the back of the house to overlook the garden, and using the freed-up space to create a children's play area. Her two children love having the run of the ground floor out into the garden, while Martha and her husband Blair take some time out to relax in this private and secluded space.

In Martha's bedroom, a striking pink vase from Absolute Flowers sits prettily against hand-printed 'Anemone' wallpaper from Neisha Crosland.

The bedroom is full of tactile furnishings, from the leather headboard of the Conran bed to the sheepskin rug by Tanya Thompson for Made. In the snug, a George Smith armchair is lit by a funky lamp from Mint.

A rosewood desk from Boom Interiors features prominently in Martha's study, where a bespoke lampshade in 'Woods' by Cole & Son contrasts with the bright Marimekko curtains.

The **B&B** Italia sofa in the sitting room is large enough for the entire family. Martha customized the coffee table by replacing the glass with a bright-pink top, while the armchair was found in the street by Martha's mum and reupholstered. There are no neutral tones in this bathroom, where an artwork has been fashioned from a **Liberty** print and the curtains from a bright sweep of fabric from **D**esigners **G**uild.

BILL AMBERG + SUSIE FORBES
QUEEN'S PARK

A leather accessories designer and a magazine editor have turned a Victorian house in Queen's Park into a stylish, contemporary home with a friendly family feel.

As a young creative couple living in London in the early 1990s, Bill Amberg and Susie Forbes wanted to be at the centre of things and chose to live on the top floor of a white stucco house in Notting Hill. Bill had just established his eponymous label, which continues the tradition of British luxury brands together with his own modern take on hand-crafted leather bags and accessories, and Susie had just joined *Vogue* as a features editor and was working closely with innovative British designers and photographers. Fifteen years on, Susie is now editor of *Easy Living* magazine and Bill's company has gone global, with stockists around the world.

Bill and Susie discovered Queen's Park through mutual friends, and despite Susie's misgivings about this 'Godforsaken part of London', they began to see the potential of moving to the area. They decided to put a note through the door of any house that they liked the look of – 'as you used to be able to do in those days,' remembers Susie. Eventually someone wanted to sell, and they bought their new home in early 1996. Their semi-detached, red-brick Victorian house had a traditional layout, with two small, dark rooms and a long hallway on the ground floor. Bill and Susie weighed up the pros and cons of keeping the period features, before deciding to open up the whole ground floor to create one light-filled room, with windows at each end. 'We worried about sacrificing the original character of the house,' Susie explains, 'but the existing layout really did feel too pokey.'

With the addition of silver metallic wallpaper, mosaic mirror tiles and Moroccan lanterns, this family house could now be a rock star's pad. In the vast ground-floor space, Bill's furniture designs, including a huge blue velvet sofa and a distressed leather console, are prominently featured alongside a Louis XIV-style three-piece suite, which the couple customized by painting white and reupholstering in soft pink fabric from the Designers Guild. The snug, where the family gathers to watch television, received its Moroccan flavour from the addition of decorative wooden cupboards, which have been painted white and given mirrored backs, and embossed leather floor tiles designed by Bill. Susie found the vivid green curtains with their pom-pom trim at the Designers Guild, and picked up the bold print cushions from Anthropologie, a favourite store in the US. Also in this ground-floor space is a small loo, where Susie has hung an iconic poster-sized *Vogue* cover featuring Kate Moss on the wall.

Bill and Susie's approach to designing the house was certainly unconventional, and they will go to great lengths to obtain bespoke pieces or customize vintage furniture, rather than buy brand-new designs. For the kitchen, they commissioned a joiner to build the units and the white shelving system, which is filled with Bill's collection of Georgian glass together with a white candelabra from The Cross, while Bill sourced the surfaces from the old St George's Hospital (now the Lanesborough Hotel). Susie, meanwhile, had seen some elegant mother-of-pearl chairs in interiors shops, but wanted to see if she could buy them directly from India. She simply typed 'twelve mother-of-pearl Indian chairs' into Google, and six months later her chairs arrived from Jodhpur. She dealt with an extremely efficient company called Art and Decorative Objects, who emailed images to her and arranged for shipping.

When it came to her daughters' bedrooms, Susie looked for unusual pieces on the Internet, or simply commissioned pieces that she couldn't find elsewhere. Instead of buying a contemporary bunk bed, Susie wanted to re-create a design she had seen in a magazine, which had the appearance of two single antique French beds stuck together, and contacted La Maison, a specialist bed company in London's East End, to come up with the look. On a trip to New York, Susie visited Anthropologie and brought home vintage-style fabric letters spelling out 'Poppy' to hang from the upper bunk. And continuing with the down-home American feel, Susie picked out some vintage floral wallpaper from an American-based website. Closer to home, she found the antique mirror and chandelier in Portobello Road. Perhaps as a concession to Bill, their own bedroom feels more restrained, with white-painted walls and floors. It is only the furry headboard and velvet ottoman in pink that add a splash of colour.

Susie speaks with dismay about chipped floorboards in the kitchen and children's graffiti on the leather bedside tables, but there is something incredibly reassuring about visiting a family home that is really lived in, as opposed to a pristine designer pad. This is a house with soul that reflects the lives of the whole family, headed by two creative parents.

Daughter Poppy's name is spelled out in fabric letters from Anthropologie in New York, against vintage wallpaper.

The leather console and blue velvet sofa in the sitting room were designed by **Bill**, while the **Louis XIV**-style chairs were customized by the couple, who painted them white and reupholstered them in pink fabric from the **Designers Guild**. **Bill**'s study overlooks the garden; the leather desk, chair and lamp are all bespoke pieces. A contemporary sideboard holds artworks by friends and family.

Susie commissioned the bunk beds in Poppy's bedroom from La Maison, while the bureau is from Bill's parents. In the kitchen, the mother-of-pearl chairs from India are placed around a table picked up on sale from Habitat. The Moroccan-style snug with its white-painted cupboards is where the family watch TV. Out in the garden, Bill's shed is filled with vintage furniture, sheepskins and tribal artefacts.

SE1, SE5 SE22, SW3,
SW6, SW7, SW9
BERMONDSEY
CAMBERWELL
EAST DULWICH
CHELSEA
PARSON'S GREEN
SOUTH KENSINGTON
BRIXTON

BOROUGH OF CHELSEA
KING'S ROAD
S.W. 3

To remove them from the wealthy areas of the City and the West End, breweries, sugar refineries, gasworks and glue factories were deliberately located south of the river. Bermondsey, home to London's tanning trade from the eighteenth century, suffered a reversal of fortunes when the industry declined throughout the 1970s. But the area is thriving once again, and former warehouses are being turned into loft-style flats and office spaces. And with the opening of the Camberwell College of Arts and the South London Gallery in the late nineteenth century, Camberwell has been a centre for contemporary art and design for well over a century. East Dulwich, too, became a smart, tree-lined suburb after the opening of its railway station in 1863.

Glitzy Chelsea has been home to royalty and the rock-'n'-roll aristocracy ever since Henry VIII first sailed down the Thames and purchased Chelsea Manor, an act which was to transform the once tiny fishing village. The riverbank Georgian terrace of Cheyne Walk later became home to artists such as Turner and Whistler, and gained further notoriety in the 1960s and '70s as the home of Keith Richards and Mick Jagger. Chelsea gained the ultimate seal of approval when it (together with Kensington) was named a Royal Borough in 1964 to commemorate the site of Queen Victoria's birth in 1819.

Worlds away from label-conscious Chelsea, Brixton was considered a suburban paradise with the opening of its own railway station in 1862, and local residents flocked to Electric Avenue (later immortalized in song by Eddy Grant), the first shopping street in South London to have electricity. But throughout the 1980s and '90s, Brixton acquired a reputation for violent crime and drugs. With the reopening of the Ritzy Cinema and a revived music scene, however, it is now one of the more exciting places to live in the capital.

SE1

NORMAN ACKROYD
BERMONDSEY

A warehouse in an historic leather-working neighbourhood in South London provides an inspiring home for an established artist.

Over the past twenty-five years, Norman Ackroyd has travelled to the extremities of the British Isles, drawing and sketching the coastline from land and sea, and then returning to his warehouse in Bermondsey to make prints and etchings of his drawings as a visual record of his journeys. Elected to the Royal Academy in 1990, Norman is represented by galleries in both the UK and America. His work has always taken priority when choosing where and how to live: in his Victorian terraced house in Clapham, for example, all of the heavy print-making machinery was stored on the ground floor. Because it was difficult to work like this in a domestic space, Norman decided to re-evaluate where he lived. He soon discovered that for the same price as his Clapham house, he could buy a castle outside Glasgow or a semi-derelict warehouse in Bermondsey.

Opting for the latter, Norman found a warehouse that offered a vast amount of space for such a central location and had huge potential. He asked the advice of one of his clients, a property surveyor, who told him that although structurally sound, there were still 'one hundred pages of faults' with the building. But Norman decided to take a chance, and in 1983 moved in with his young family. Because the house was built as a leather warehouse in 1846, before the era of steel supports and concrete foundations, its internal construction is made up of solid wood beams and floorboards, and it comes as a shock to see a wooden column holding up the whole structure. Norman believes that the wood beams were preserved by the leather tanning, as the hides would have been stored on shelves in the roof beams and trusses. Although the leather industry is no longer at the heart of Bermondsey, street names such as Leathermarket, Tanner and Morocco still remain. 'I used to go running up by the river early in the morning and pass by all the spice warehouses, with the fantastic smell of roasting spices,' recalls Norman. 'All that has gone now, but you still find places such as Cinnamon Wharf.'

Before the family was allowed to move in, the council insisted on the installation of a two-storey, stainless-steel fire stair and the separation of Norman's basement work area, with its highly flammable materials, from the rest of the building. No one had ever lived in the warehouse before, giving Norman complete freedom over the building's look and design, but the drawback was that it had no central heating or hot water. 'I come from a family that has always lived above the shop,' explains Norman. 'My father was a butcher, so in a way it's in the blood.' The family had to camp out on the first floor and try to stay warm until the building work was finished. The builders set to work on the upper floors to replace the damaged floorboards and repair the roof. Norman wanted to leave all of the plumbing and central heating pipes deliberately on show, to encourage the builders to do really beautiful work. All of the new wiring runs along the top of the beams, making it virtually invisible. The roof lights were installed in 2005, and Norman loves them: 'They give me this wonderful pool of light in the middle of the room. It's just a beautiful place in which to work watercolour.'

Once the building works were complete, the top floor of the warehouse became one huge open-plan living space, with exposed roof beams, perfect for both family games and entertaining. 'I bought two dozen live lobsters, huge things from Billingsgate, and piles of prawns and crayfish,' remembers Norman. 'We put a massive table right in the middle of the room and had a huge party.' Norman placed an antique wooden dresser against the bare brick wall of the kitchen, which he customized by adding wooden shelves above and rows of wine boxes along the base for extra storage. He was keen to find a compromise between keeping the feel of an open-plan warehouse and creating a sense of privacy in his bedroom. The bedroom area has a glass roof, and Norman has devised a four-poster structure around the bed with sliding canvas screens to block out the light. French double doors open out onto a small roof terrace, which offers views over Bermondsey High Street and Zandra Rhodes' bright-pink-and-orange Fashion Museum. There are several different work areas arranged on this floor, depending on what Norman is working on. Plan chests have been turned into useful workspaces for painting and drawing, and paints, brushes and bottles are stored in old wooden wine boxes arranged on shelves along the landing.

'When I first moved to Bermondsey, there were still places in the area that were curing, preparing and dying hides,' recalls Norman, 'but the whole area was completely run-down and derelict.' With the decline of leather industry, many of the old warehouses in Bermondsey were converted into loft-style flats and offices. Only Norman's warehouse, with its huge open-plan spaces and industrial furniture, has remained relatively untouched, providing a link to the area's industrial past.

Detail of artist Norman Ackroyd's watercolour palette.

The double doors of the top-floor sitting room were originally
designed to allow hides to be delivered via the cast-iron winch
outside. At the kitchen table, Norman surveys the works-in-progress.

An industrial crane was needed to lift Norman's grand piano onto the top-floor terrace before it could be carried through to the sitting room. Paints and brushes line the corridors, while DIY materials are stored in a vintage plan chest. In the kitchen, custom-built shelves keep everything on display and vintage wine cases double up as storage. Elsewhere, photos and sketches provide inspiration.

When the sun is shining, the roof terrace acts as a sun trap, and Norman opens out the double doors to the surrounding rooftops and the cityscape beyond. Even the bathroom has a magnificent view, following the line of houses backing onto Bermondsey High Street. In the bedroom, the wooden four-poster bed's sliding canvas panels removes the necessity for blinds or curtains to block out the light.

PEGGY PRENDEVILLE CAMBERWELL

An Arts and Crafts chapel in Camberwell is brought into the twenty-first century via a sensitive conversion enhanced by contemporary design.

Interior designer Peggy Prendeville specializes in conversions of factories and warehouses, and had been looking for an industrial-type space to turn into a family home. She heard about a chapel in Camberwell through a developer who himself specialized in unusual spaces. 'I kept telling him that I was too busy to look at the chapel,' remembers Peggy. 'It makes me cringe to think that I could have lost out on it.' In recent years, the chapel had been part of Goldsmiths College; Peggy's art-critic husband Tony Godfrey had given lectures here, and many of their friends had passed through the building as students. The building was attached to a hall-of-residence, which had originally been built as a teacher-training college for Christian ladies (St Gabriel's) by Arts and Crafts architect Philip Appleby Robson in 1903.

All of the plans for the Grade II-listed building had to be approved by English Heritage. Rather than trying to re-create the chapel's original interiors, Peggy was encouraged to go for a modern glass structure. 'It was fun to go against my normal sensibility,' recalls Peggy, 'because it makes you think very hard about to how to approach the project.' She followed the planning criteria by making sure that all changes could be easily reversible, and chose not to divide the rooms with stud walls, instead using wooden cupboards that were fitted together with intricate joinery. Peggy loves the Latin lettering that runs around the top of the chapel walls, and used lots of glass for balustrading and shelving to preserve the transparency of the space.

Peggy's previous schemes favoured small bedrooms and large living spaces, but she turned this upside-down when she ended up with a huge open-plan bedroom beneath the chapel roof. Even the bed was designed to be a specific height beneath the lettering on the wall: 'I like to have modern things that contrast to the old building in a sensitive way,' she explains. The customized bed was made from chocolate-brown leather squares, and the blanket box, hand-lacquered in China, was designed to perfectly line up with them. Perhaps the most luxurious addition was a free-standing bath from Bathstore, wrapped in deep-brown faux snakeskin.

Having trained as an artist and illustrator, Peggy has a painterly approach to colour. Instead of imitating the original green-and-red colour scheme around the altarpiece, she chose a deep aubergine for the contemporary screen behind it. Peggy had admired the work of Mark Brazier-Jones for years, but his furniture had never quite worked within her loft conversions. As soon as she bought the chapel, she was straight on the phone to Brazier-Jones and ended up commissioning a couple of chairs, a desk and a dining table from the designer, which they collaborated on together. Instead of replacing the old farmhouse kitchen, her builder suggested re-cladding the old doors with polished stainless steel, which acts as a mirror. 'It felt sacrilegious to use the altar for our kitchen,' admits Peggy, 'but our excuse was that the previous owner did it, and we just inherited it!' The high-backed velvet sofas were designed to be the same height as the kitchen worktop, because Peggy was worried that conventionally low sofas would make the room feel like an airport lounge.

Living areas and bedrooms are hidden behind church pews and an ornate carved wooden screen that stands at one end of the chapel. Peggy wanted to balance out the design by creating a gallery area at the opposite end, just above the altarpiece. A narrow staircase is only 500mm wide because it was essential that it did not take up too much floor space and conceal the intricate design of the marble floor beneath. Peggy feels that this gallery area is closest to her usual designs, and consequently it is her favourite space in the house. It is beautifully lit to display favourite artworks, including a sculpture by Portuguese artist Graça Pereira Coutinho and ceramic vases by Mary Barclay. Looking across the chapel, there is a fabulous view of three pictures on the first floor, arranged in a row above the balustrade, by John Walker, Coutinho and Ian McKeever.

How to combine old and new is one of the most talked about aspects of design, but also one of the most difficult to achieve. With Peggy's experience of warehouse and factory conversions, she brought a fresh approach to this early twentieth-century chapel. Having learnt about traditional building techniques from English Heritage, she combined them with her love of contemporary design. Rather than filling the chapel with heavy Victorian pieces or Arts and Crafts furniture, Peggy has picked out the best of modern design from Saporetti and Missoni, as well as from Brazier-Jones. This family has always lived together in open-plan spaces, and seem to thrive on living in unusual buildings.

The striking inlaid marble flooring of the chapel, which dates back to the turn of the twentieth century.

Peggy strolls past her husband's second-floor library, echoing the dynamic pose of the photograph above her. The altarpiece had already been converted into a kitchen by the previous owner.

Behind the original wooden pews, a glass screen conceals the bedroom belonging to Peggy's teenage daughter. A stone spiral staircase leads from the front door to the main living space, where Peggy opted for contemporary furniture rather than attempting any kind of pastiche. The fleur-de-lis walls and intricate flooring of the chapel make a bold contrast to the new gallery.

Concealed behind the screen is a slim staircase made purposefully narrow to avoid covering the marble floor. In the gallery are Peggy's favourite artworks, along with a **Saporetti** chair upholstered in **Missoni** fabric and a glass coffee table from **B&B Italia**. The bedroom and bathroom are tucked under the wooden roof beams on the third floor; the bespoke, hand-lacquered blanket box is from **China**.

ERIN O'CONNOR
CAMBERWELL

A fashion model's Georgian home in South London receives a stylish update via a fruitful collaboration with an interiors designer.

During her successful twelve-year career as an in-demand fashion model, Erin O'Connor had lived in New York and Notting Hill before deciding to buy this Georgian terraced house in Camberwell in 2005. 'It was a deliberate move,' she explains. 'Once I cross the bridge to South London, I feel free of my work image.' She was attracted to her new neighbourhood because of its studenty feel and the suggestion that anything could happen. As the face of Marks & Spencer, Erin had met interiors stylist Suzy Hoodless on a shoot and loved her style: 'I remembered her interiors as a little slice of heaven, where Suzy had just pulled everything together in 30 seconds, and made it look lived-in and stylish.' Having bought her Grade II-listed house in March, work began, with Suzy's help, the following September. Suzy, too, could immediately see the building's potential: 'It was such a handsome house, and had fantastic proportions and structure.'

Erin herself says: 'Initially it was more about what we were going to take away. Once you start stripping a house of its former personality, it's easier to decide what to do next.' Rather than letting Erin search for vintage furniture on her own, Suzy accompanied her to auction houses around the country and to specialist antiques dealers. Suzy and her client measured out each room and even borrowed furniture to see how it would fit, so that there was no chance of making a mistake. 'We had a lot of fun choosing the furniture, and I've been educated via Suzy,' Erin freely admits. 'But I don't know that I would have been brave enough without her to bring it up-to-date in a way that was modern, without compromising the traditional style of the house.'

Throughout the building are portraits of Erin by the artists and photographers that she has worked with over the past decade. 'Sometimes clients ask if I would like to be paid in money or in art, and I would rather invest in the art as a reminder of the work I've done,' she says. Looking at the drawings and photographs around the house, she feels, 'is like a diary of when and where I was in each instance.' Every room in the house has a dedicated theme and mood, and the girls collected up vintage finds to suit the feel of each different space. The basement kitchen is probably the most experimental room, as it mixes teacup-print wallpaper with antique cases full of butterflies and a floral sofa. Suzy encouraged Erin to be bold (wallpaper can easily be painted over), to give the room a completely different feel to the rest of the house. 'The kitchen is quite social and seems to be a place where people gravitate to naturally,' says Erin. 'It's a real hub of the house.'

The ground-floor room was designed to be a cool and restful environment, with linen-covered sofas, Hessian blinds and rugs made from palm leaves. Suzy tried to imagine the kind of furniture that might have been here in the late eighteenth and early nineteenth centuries, and chose a couple of Chesterfield sofas, a wing-backed armchair and a classic Georgian three-legged table. She mixed these up with a French floor lamp from the 1940s, which was spray-painted a deep orangey-red, and a bold pair of antlers to pick up on the organic, natural feel of the room. There are even two glass 'cabinets of curiosities', filled with odd, interesting bits collected by Suzy and Erin, from antique leather books to tiny taxidermy birds from Dover Street Market and a vintage crown.

One consequence of Erin's job is that she had so many clothes that she had to turn one of the largest rooms in the house into her dressing room. Here, Suzy wanted the wardrobe doors to look as invisible as possible, and disguised them with a geometric-print wallpaper. She ordered the neon yellow rug from The Rug Company, and dyed some lace fabric midnight-blue to screen the windows overlooking the street. The dressing table is made from a camera case on tripod legs, with a transparent chair by Philippe Starck. By contrast, Erin's small bedroom is painted a soft, dusky lilac, with a hand-painted headboard and vintage textiles on the bed. At the top of the house, an attic room is a cosy, womb-like space: 'This is where you want to flop at the end of the day. On the weekends, I am hard pushed to leave this room, and if I do it's just to collect the newspapers.' Suzy had an L-shaped deep-green velvet sofa made for the space, which doubles up as a sofa bed for extra guests. All of the cushions were made from vintage textiles or hand-embroidered designs from Colefax & Fowler.

Because she travels constantly for work, Erin was desperate to put down roots and couldn't wait to move into her new home in Camberwell, where she has close friends living nearby. Erin ended up selling the few bits of furniture that she had, as they looked chunky and oversized in her small house, and started again from scratch. Through working with Suzy, Erin has created a quirky and original home that reflects her own distinctive personality.

Pinned to the wall of Erin's dressing room are a worn pair of ballet shoes, from her regular practice sessions in the studios of the Royal Ballet Company. The wallpaper is an original Suzy Hoodless design.

Erin and Suzy had this discontinued teacup-print wallpaper specially reproduced and, after initially deciding to paper only one wall, went ahead and covered each wall of the cosy, retro kitchen. The sitting room mixes nineteenth-century design with contemporary pieces, such as this vivid orange Serge Morris lamp from the 1940s. A high window ledge provides a sunny spot for a bit of birdwatching.

In the dressing room, **Suzy** designed the wardrobe doors to be as invisible as possible, hidden behind a delicate wallpaper design. Windows are screened for privacy with strips of antique lace, dyed midnight blue. The dressing table, made from a black aluminium camera case with tripod legs, looks as if it would be at home on a film set; pulled up to it is a 'Ghost' chair by **Philippe Starck**.

ROB + JOSIE DA BANK
EAST DULWICH

Music and travel are the influences behind this comfortable family home in a leafy South London neighbourhood.

Having founded Sunday Best in 1995, DJ Rob da Bank took the club to Ibiza in 2001, where it became the first weekly chill-out on the island, and subsequently played on the Glastonbury stage. Rob and his wife Josie, who met at college when they were just eighteen and have lived and worked together ever since, decided to combine their skills and start their own festival (called 'Bestival') on the Isle of Wight in 2004. 'We started Bestival because we've got the same kind of vision of things,' explains Rob. 'Bestival is a marriage of my love of music and Josie's design sense.' Four years later and the headline acts include artists such as the Beastie Boys, the Chemical Brothers and Primal Scream. As Rob says, 'a lot of people have the best weekend of their lives at Bestival, they get married and bring their babies, meet friends who they are now best friends with. People have life-changing experiences there.'

Rob and Josie moved to East Dulwich in South London in 2002, the same year that Rob joined BBC's Radio 1 as a DJ. Their house is set along a crescent and the walls are not quite straight, but the couple love the quirky, unusual feel of their home. This was no ordinary house, as there was a spaceship in the garden and a bed fitted into the triangular space of the roof. Rob's approach to renovating the house was to go away on holiday and get someone else to do all the work: stripping the Anaglypta off the walls; sanding the floorboards and painting them white; and putting in a new kitchen. When they first moved in, the couple had very few possessions, and their main priority was to find somewhere to store Rob's records. The triangular attic bedroom turned out to be the perfect studio for Rob, who just slotted shelves into the alcoves for his LPs. One year later, the pair set off travelling to hunt down quirky finds for their home. They brought back vintage posters from the 1950s for a Polish circus in Australia, along with Bollywood posters from a junk shop in Udaipur that now adorn the walls of their son Arlo's bedroom.

Artist-turned-textile designer Josie loves mixing colour and texture, such as Marimekko prints with Indian textiles, and made most of the cushions and curtains for the house. She now designs all of the brightly coloured tents for Bestival, which are decorated with vintage lamps and fabric. Rob jokes that moving into their house was the beginning of Josie's furniture museum, as she is continually bringing home vintage pieces that she has found in the junk shops and antiques shops surrounding their house. She picked up the sideboard for the sitting room for a bargain £160 (down from £500), and found the yellow dresser and wooden bench, now piled high with Indian cushions, from a local shop called Carrier.

The couple are drawn to one-off designs, and many of the more unusual items in the house were presents from Rob to Josie, such as the lamp in the shape of a pineapple, the knitted cakes on the cake stand in the sitting room, and the lion's head on the wall. The sitting-room walls are covered with pictures in vintage frames, a combination of presents from friends and junk-shop finds. Josie discovered the picture of an oil rig in a skip, found a portrait of Gandhi from a night market in India, and picked up prints from charity shops. The comfortable velvet sofa covered with cushions from Morocco and India is from Habitat.

An Indian papier-mâché cow's head hung with garlands hangs at the top of the white-painted wooden stairs, leading through to the bathroom. Josie felt that this room could do with a makeover and bought sheets of mirrored mosaic tiles and a rug from Cath Kidston to brighten it up. For the bedroom, she chose a Neisha Crosland hand-printed wallpaper in muted tones of grey, and found some antique Indian pencil drawings to hang on the walls. The antique French bed is from a shop round the corner in Lordship Lane, and the chandelier, too, was bought locally, but the bedcover is from Jaipur. Sadly, as East Dulwich becomes ever more gentrified, Josie has noticed that more and more of the antiques shops that she has frequented over the years have closed down.

The house has been the starting point for many of Rob and Josie's creative endeavours, from working on Bestival together around the kitchen table to inspiring Josie's designs for lampshades and curtains, and even the creation of Rob's music studio under the eaves. Having spent so many years travelling and working, they both love spending time at home, and feel that they have created a space that perfectly reflects their love of Bollywood, Moroccan style and music festivals.

A knitted monkey belonging to the couple's son Arlo rests on a hand-embroidered throw from Pakistan.

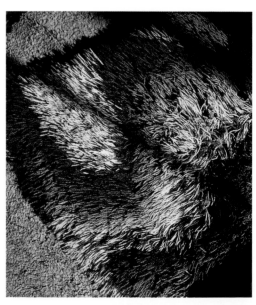

Eclectic decorative details throughout the home include a lampshade fashioned by Josie and a lion's head (sporting a tiny top hat) purchased from a shop in **Notting Hill** – Arlo is convinced that it is a real lion! In the sitting room, an wooden bench picked up in **Kerala**, in southwestern India, is topped with cushions hand-made by Josie from vintage **Rajasthani** textiles.

Sheets of mirrored mosaic tiles from **Tile & Stone Magic** and a rug from **Cath Kidston** glam up the bathroom, while in Arlo's room, a hand-embroidered throw and a blue-painted wardrobe add warmth and colour. In the sitting room, Josie's own artwork is displayed above a velvet sofa from **Habitat**, which is customized with bright cushions acquired during the couple's travels in **Morocco** and **India**.

Ceci n'est pas une pipe.

Josie loves the muted colours of the Neisha Crosland wallpaper in her bedroom, and when she found some antique Indian pencil drawings on crumbling pieces of paper, she thought they would work perfectly against the walls. A yellow-painted dresser holds such treasured gifts as a pineapple lamp with a Hawaiian shade, a cake stand with knitted cupcakes, and a mirror that was Josie's thirtieth birthday present.

SW3

TRACEY BOYD
CHELSEA

A fashion designer and a former pop star take a hands-on approach to this mews house in Chelsea, which combines vintage nostalgia with modern design.

Designer Tracey Boyd's fashion collections are known for being feminine without being too girly, and for appealing to women with an individual sense of style – from model Lily Cole to actresses Keira Knightley and Kirsten Dunst. Tracey set up her fashion label in 1996, and from the beginning has worked closely with her partner Adrian Wright, who assists with every aspect of the business (Adrian was part of legendary band The Human League in the 1980s; possessing no musical skills to speak of, he was appointed their 'Director of Visuals'!).

Having bought their Chelsea mews house in 2002, the couple recognized that it was always going to be a challenge to live together – Tracey loves romantic antique pieces, while Adrian prefers clean, contemporary design. But Adrian also wanted to create a house with soul, where nothing looked too new or too perfect. The white-painted floor, for example, is made from soft planks of wood, roughly sanded and nailed down. It does get scuffed and worn, but this is exactly the effect he was after. Adrian refuses to subscribe to the current notion that good design is only possible at a high price. All of the metal door handles in the kitchen and the aluminium coat hooks in the hallway were picked up in Paris flea markets for one Euro each – proving his point that it's often cheaper to find original designs from a street market than to go to Ikea or John Lewis. 'Adrian's opened my eyes to the 1930s, '50s and '60s,' explains Tracey, 'while I've opened up his to more antiquey things and decorative pieces.'

To divide up the ground-floor space, the couple built a low platform at the back of the room for the dining table, chairs and writing desk. The rosewood table and chairs are Danish designs from the 1950s; Adrian rescued the chairs from a skip and the table is from a car boot sale. An antique chandelier from Rainbow in Fulham hangs above the dining table and catches the light reflected off the sequined rug from Morocco, while the ornate writing desk, which belonged to Tracey's grandmother, makes a great contrast to Adrian's Modernist pieces. A comfortable seating area is defined with a soft, green sofa from the Designers Guild and a vintage

coffee table customized by Adrian. It was originally a wooden card table with curved legs and a leather top, but Adrian cut the legs in half and replaced the leather with bevelled glass to create a unique table that still has the pull-out drawers and places for drinks of the old card table. Bookshelves against the wall, built by Adrian and facing the street, ensure that the couple aren't overlooked, while a row of skylights light up the room. To more clearly mark out the kitchen as a separate part of the room, Adrian and Tracey painted it green and built a glass wall to break up the open-plan space. They have chosen not to have any drawers in the kitchen, and instead store pots and pans behind vintage-print curtains and utensils in jugs on the counter.

A white-painted staircase leads to the bedroom, bathroom and dressing room on the first floor. The bedroom has a romantic feel, with its wooden French bed placed beneath an antique chandelier. Even the wardrobe and chest of drawers look like antique pieces, but they are actually junk-shop finds customized by Adrian. To protect the old bed and its hand-carved roses, Adrian has placed an Ikea bed frame within it and installed a comfortable latex mattress. Tracey picked out the heart-shaped mirrors and porcelain flowers to create a more feminine feel. In keeping with the romantic mood, Adrian painted a child's wardrobe white and lined it with fabric to make an elegant jewelry box for Tracey. A Victorian door, cut in half, separates the bedroom from the bathroom; the couple added porcelain door handles and replaced the panels with glass. With its sloping ceiling and roof light, the cosy, wood-panelled bathroom feels like a French garret. The standard bath has been wood panelled especially to fit the room. Adrian also found a unique 1930s porcelain soap dish, which can be suspended over the bath like a shelf. To create more storage, Adrian built cupboards beneath the overhanging roof. The couple reupholstered a chaise longue, which opens up like a trunk, found in a junk shop, and made cushions from antique French floral fabric.

Tracey and Adrian have spent the past twenty years travelling together and looking for quirky pieces for their home. As she tries to explain this need to collect, Tracey says: 'The excitement is in finding something different, rather than having something new to take home. Even something ugly can be placed in such a way that it looks quirky and attractive.' Despite the couple's differences, Tracey feels that 'a lot of the little things that we actually buy are things that we both really love.'

A selection of antique books that belonged to Tracey's grandmother are displayed next to a Scandinavian vase from the 1950s.

Adrian found the 1950s dining chairs in a skip and bought the rosewood table for £15 from a car boot sale. In the sitting room, a soft green sofa in a Modernist design is from the Designers Guild, while the 1950s-style chair is from Habitat and the 1970s G-Plan footstool was picked up from a flea market in New York. To unify the look, both pieces were reupholstered in 'Polka Peony' fabric designed by Tracey.

To create a separate kitchen area, Tracey and Adrian installed a glass partition and painted the room a favourite shade of green. The door handles and hinges are from specialist shops in Paris, and all of the crockery is from a Parisian flea market. In the bathroom, a bath tucked into the eaves, cushions made from French floral fabric, and a chaise longue from a junk shop in Newcastle add to the cosy feel.

Tracey's dressing table came from an antiques shop in Lillie Road, in Fulham, which the couple customized with a mirrored top and a 1950s moonlight mirror from Alfies Antique Market, which has Perspex flowers around the edge that light up. The couple bought their French bed from Judy Greenwood nearly twenty-five years ago; it is painted grey and white, and each one of the hand-carved roses is different.

SW6

ANNABEL DEARLOVE
PARSON'S GREEN

Japanese influences and ultra-modern materials lead the way in this architect-designed house in the heart of Parson's Green.

Annabel and Mark Dearlove bought their house at the western end of the King's Road in 1999, and within a few months were talking to architect Nick Helm about how to alter the building to accommodate their growing family. The couple love to entertain and wanted to create an open-plan ground-floor space, where they could gather friends and family together, but at the same time, having looked at lots of narrow London townhouses, they also knew that they didn't want to live in a top-heavy house. When they had the chance to extend into the garden, Annabel and Mark instinctively felt that this could be the perfect solution.

The architect had worked with interior designer Maria Speake of architectural salvage firm Retrouvius on previous projects, and was keen to collaborate with her again (for Maria's own house, see p. 168). Their ambitious plans revolved around connecting the original Georgian house to the mews house behind. The aim was to link the two buildings by creating a new structure in the garden, wrapped around a small courtyard area. It took three long years to get planning permission before work could begin in 2002, and another two years before it was completed. 'We wanted to create a glass skylight to bring light into the depth of the building,' explains Maria, 'rather than designing a glass-box extension which can often be too hot and bright during the day, and turn into a cold vacuum at night.'

The hallway leading from the main house to the new extension ends with a small door that opens onto a double-height door lined with lilac felt, which acts as a quirky reminder of the traditional green baize door that used to divide the servants' quarters from the rest of the house. In this case, the door marks the contrast between the Georgian structure and the twenty-first century addition. The new extension can now accommodate the whole family, whether lounging on L-shaped sofas from B&B Italia or sat around the kitchen table – designed by Maria – that overlooks the courtyard garden. Glass doors leading to the kitchen and dining room concertina back to create an outdoor room during the summer months. Having spent six years living in Japan in the 1990s, the Dearlove family wanted to bring a little of the Far East into their home. Maria commissioned a Japanese-inspired tree-branch design in dusty pink from Timorous Beasties, to be used on cushions and blinds throughout the house, and as an artwork on the long wall behind the dining table. (The print has proved so popular that it has now gone into production!) Picking up on the theme, the courtyard garden is planted with a cherry tree and Japanese grasses, which change from pink to green during the year, with seasonal red berries. The copper-coloured bark of the cherry tree also works beautifully with the bespoke copper and bronze metalwork in the courtyard.

Inside the house, Maria chose to work only with reclaimed wood and hand-poured concrete in a variety of textures and finishes: 'I used reclaimed oak in its various forms, with very wide boards used for the dining-room floor and big chunky pieces for the table,' she says. Concrete was used for both structural support and to fashion elegant, polished work surfaces and floor tiles. Where concrete is used structurally, Maria chose a sand aggregate mix to create a rough texture that would contrast with the smoother surfaces. The warm colours and materials used throughout the house were inspired by a visit to the 2001 Vermeer exhibition at the National Gallery: 'I became obsessed,' recalls Maria, 'and picked up on the idea of using tiles throughout the house.' She commissioned a muted palette of glazed tiles from Agnes Amery in Belgium, complemented by corresponding paint colours in dense, pigment-rich shades. The dining room and sitting room are on different levels, and a sleek concrete desk – topped with a smooth surface in pink leather – has been slotted into the space next to stairs that separate the two rooms, with shelves of books within easy reach.

Upstairs, Annabel's study is located in a gallery overlooking the kitchen and courtyard garden, so that she can have some privacy while still feeling connected to the activities within the house. The gallery leads to the bedroom, with its wooden platform bed and Japanese-inspired display of grasses in vintage ceramic vases. Brightly painted silkscreens have been lit from behind to create innovative artworks, and teak salvaged from the old Queen Charlotte's Hospital in Goldhawk Road has been used for shelving and to create a desk area.

This collaboration between Nick Helm, Maria Speake and the Dearloves has resulted in an environmentally friendly home, created using recycled oak and teak. The unique space combines contemporary furniture from B&B Italia with 1960s designs from Hans Wegner, among others, to create a new modern classic.

Vintage glass vases from Denmark hold a display of Japanese grasses.

Both the kitchen table, surrounded with chairs by Hans Wegner, and the long dining table, with its leather chairs by Fellini, were made from planks of reclaimed oak. Above the dining table is a Japanese-inspired print, a bespoke design from Timorous Beasties. Throughout the house, smooth concrete has been used to create shelving and furniture, while rough textured walls define structural elements.

SW6

A cherry tree in the courtyard garden bespeaks the house's Eastern influences, whereas the luxurious minimalist style of the sitting room is offset with cushions from **Timorous Beasties** and **B&B Italia** sofas.

SW7

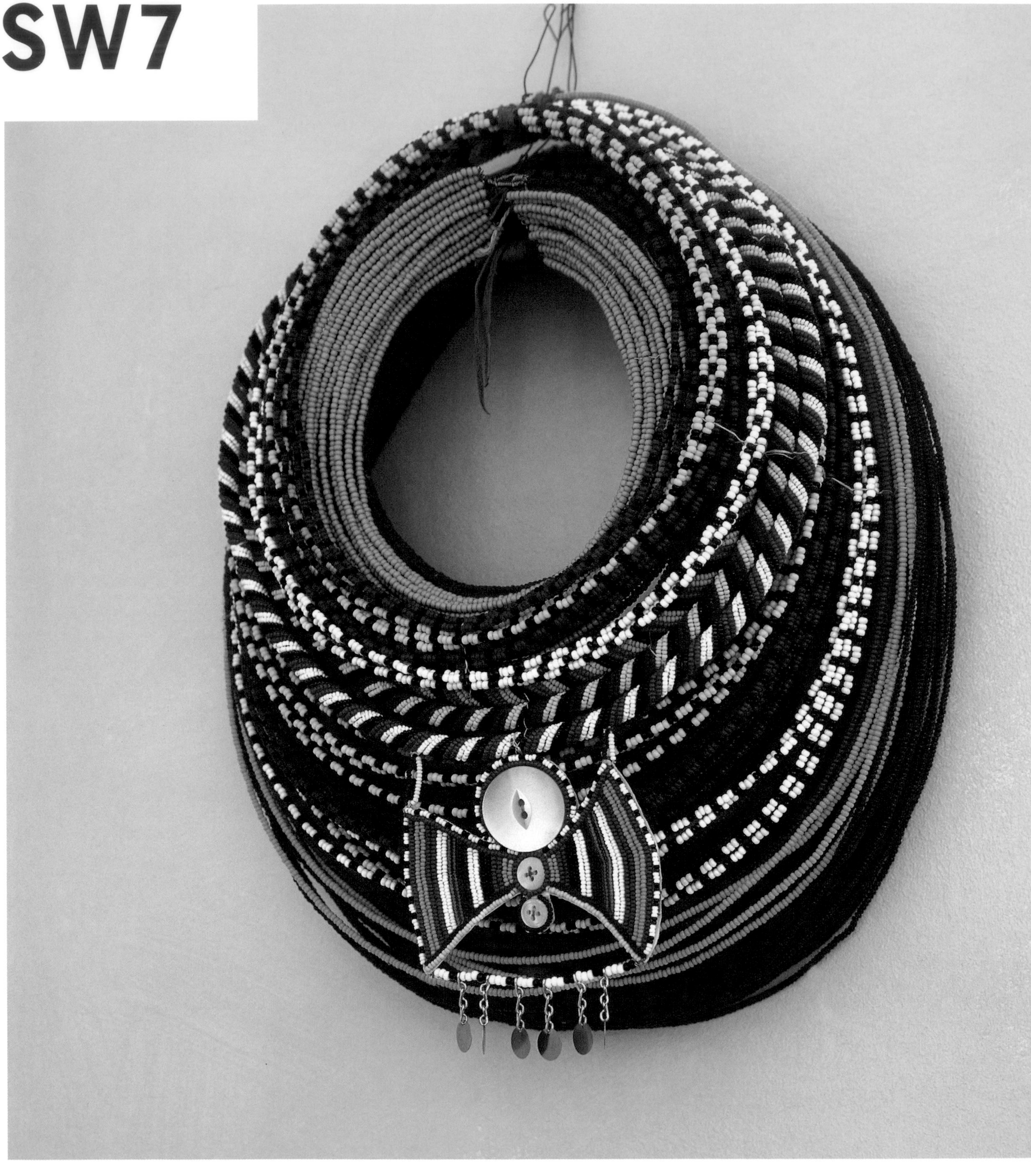

ANNABEL LEWIS
SOUTH KENSINGTON

Walls, lampshades, chandeliers and furniture all receive the luxe and beribboned V.V. Rouleaux touch in this sumptuous first-floor flat in South Kensington.

Little over a year after moving her family into a nondescript first-floor flat in South Kensington, Annabel Lewis has managed to stamp the signature style of her famous ribbons and trimmings shop, V.V. Rouleaux, onto every corner of the building. And despite having only just moved in, she's already looking to move upstairs to an apartment with more light and better views.

Annabel has painted every single room in the apartment herself, from the trompe l'oeil bamboo in the kitchen to the bright sherbet lemon in the hallway, and even the elegant designs on the sitting-room walls. Lampshades have been wrapped with ribbon from V.V. Rouleaux and brass chandeliers have been customized with gold cord and hung with tassels. Her approach to design can be summarized as: 'If I can't find it, I'll make it myself!' Fashion goes in phases, says Annabel, and the current trend is for embellishment. As she explains, 'all of the contemporary designs are completely trimmed and flowered up.' Designers such as Julien Macdonald, Paul Smith, Matthew Williamson (for Matthew's own house, see p. 22) and Alice Temperley spend hours in her warehouse, looking for inspiration among the vintage fabrics and ribbons.

Annabel likes to start with a neutral backdrop, such as wooden flooring or white walls, and then add colour and texture by embellishing and customizing the furniture and lighting. 'This sort of decorating is busy,' she declares with relish. 'It's certainly not minimalist, its maximalist!' Her favourite colour is the acid sherbet lemon, which appears over and again in the flat, perhaps to most striking effect in the hallway. When this space was painted cream, it looked 'dead and boring'. But now, says Annabel, 'it looks like the sun is shining.' With the sitting room stretching across the width of the building, Annabel decided that the perfect way to divide it to create a dining area was to suspend an antique chandelier curtain from the ceiling, which sparkles as it catches the light. The surface of the dining table was customized with wire-edged ribbon made into flattened rose shapes, which Annabel has covered with a round piece of glass to protect the design.

The centrepiece is a pressed-tin Chinese hat, worn to celebrate the Year of the Pig in 2007. To brighten up the walls around the fireplace, Annabel painted designs on backdrop paper with her friend Kate Sissons, a paint specialist, and then made a stylish oval frame for the mirror using old leaves from a French jewelry shop, glass studs and a vintage trim from 1790.

Sofas and chairs in the sitting room are upholstered in 1920s millinery velvet, which Annabel chose for its vibrant colours and vivid sheen. In order to find exactly the right shade, she will often commission velvet, screen-printed by hand, from a company in Kent or buy silk cloth from a specialist mill in Suffolk. In the bedroom, the focus is on the magnificent tented bed, a throwback to Annabel's childhood when she hankered after a romantic bedroom with a flowing canopy over the bed. Her husband Richard gets furious when he becomes tangled up in all of the ribbon, but Annabel is free to live out her fantasy. 'I just made a canopy with bits of silk and ribbon,' she says, 'and a silk taffeta bedspread in the most exquisite colours: dark chocolate brown with champagne, and then pinstripes of lime, yellow and rust.' She even customized the lampshades beside the bed by wrapping ribbon around them, a process which she claims only took half an hour.

Annabel's passion for decorating is shared by Richard, who jointly runs the V.V. Rouleaux business with her. She has an impressive sang-froid about the studs of her teenage children's jeans ripping the vintage velvet sofas in the sitting room, claiming to like the distressed effect. Her belief is that furniture can always be improved upon or customized, and there is no point becoming too hung up on just one look. Annabel is constantly updating her furniture and her surroundings: whenever she moves, all that she takes with her is the kitchen sideboard and dining table. 'Everything else is replaceable,' she says.

Hanging in the sherbet-lemon hallway is a beaded design from Kenya that was a present to Annabel from her friend Sama.

The curtain is made from antique glass, and designed to divide the dining room from the living area. Annabel teamed up with her friend Kim to paint an elegant design onto plain backdrop paper in the sitting room, and the pair made a mirror using leaves from a French jewelry shop, glass studs and vintage trim. Annabel customized the chandelier by wrapping it in gold cord and adding decorative tassels.

The chair was reupholstered in millinery velvet from the 1920s and finished off with vintage trimmings. Annabel made the canopy over the bed with bits of silk and ribbon, and the bedspread, too, is made from silk taffeta and vintage ribbon, also from the 1920s. Even the lampshades were wrapped in ribbon and beaded Indian trim from Annabel's shop, V.V. Rouleaux.

The upholstery for the sitting-room furniture is bespoke, from the screen-printed velvet for the sofa to the striking purple fabric used to cover the armchairs. The gilt mirror above the mantelpiece is from Judy Greenwood. Annabel collects trimmings and decorative objects from markets and trade fairs in Paris and New York, all of which work together to create a unique London home.

TOBIT ROCHE + NANCY OAKLEY
BRIXTON

In this Victorian townhouse in a rough South London neighbourhood, Indian textiles, African prints and family heirlooms steeped in Bloomsbury nostalgia lend a stylishly vintage feel.

Tobit Roche and Nancy Oakley moved into their Brixton house in 1993 and considered it the height of luxury; their previous home, Tobit's modest, white-painted house that Nancy had moved into twelve years previously, had no television or central heating. Now Tobit works from his artist's studio at home, while Nancy is a fashion PR director, only giving free rein to her creative side when she comes home in the evenings. The couple frequently have friends round for dinner parties, which might include drinking from antique goblets or making your own salt cellar to take home with you.

Here in Brixton, says Nancy, 'when I walk in the door, I feel like I'm in the countryside. You can come in out of the madness and walk out into the garden.' The soft colours throughout the house pick up on this gentle atmosphere: there are no hard edges or white-painted walls, and instead the couple chose to cover their staircase with kilims and paint the walls a pale sage green. In their twenty-five years together, Tobit and Nancy have amassed a unique collection of art and antiques from their travels. The painter Duncan Grant was a close friend of Tobit's father, the poet Paul Roche (Tobit lived at Charleston, Grant's home in Sussex with Vanessa Bell, for two years), and something of this bohemian and artistic collective spirit seems to have rubbed off on his own home.

The couple were keen to create an Arts and Crafts feel in their bedroom, and picked out an inlaid oak bed, a large antique armoire and a velvet Victorian armchair. Against the walls are Tobit's paintings of mountain ranges, including some inspired by the Himalayas with a peculiar sense of perspective, and a painting by Duncan Grant of the pond at Charleston. On the floor above is a tiny bedroom tucked into the eaves, with a wooden bateau-lit bed covered with a deep-green-and-red velvet throw by Georgina von Etzdorf and cushions made with antique fabric from specialist dealer Joss Graham. Behind the bed is a painting by family friend Mary Liddle, very much inspired by Odilon Redon and nicknamed 'banana fingers' by the family. It was impossible to carry a wardrobe up to this bedroom, so they had one built in-situ and

painted it pale blue. This is where Nancy stores all of her fashion treasures, including the fringed yellow Yves Saint Laurent bag that hangs from the door handle.

Even the bathroom walls are covered with an array of artworks, such as the image of the Hindu goddess Kali, picked up from an antiques shop in Delhi, and a watery reflection of a river bank, another painting by Grant. Tobit and Nancy's travels to India have influenced every aspect of their home, from Tobit's own paintings of Rajasthan to Nancy's collection of textiles. Behind the glass door of a wooden bathroom cabinet is an embroidered map of India, which Nancy bought from a craft stall in Delhi in 1986. When she went back, twenty years later the stall was still there – and only the names on the map had changed, from Bombay to Mumbai!

The sitting room is a place for the family's best-loved possessions, from their daughter's piano to Tobit's abstract paintings and Nancy's vintage textiles, including an Ottoman coat which she turned into cushions for the velvet sofa from George Smith, and a kilim fabric from Iraq that has been backed with French linen to make stylish curtains. An armchair covered with striped, hand-woven fabric from Morocco has been placed next to the mantelpiece, while the chair opposite is covered with an Indian throw, made from dip-dyed black fabric with a gold stripe. A glass-fronted cabinet displays yet more family treasures: goblets from the Aldermaston pottery; photographs of Paul Roche; and portraits of the couple's two children, Duncan and India.

The kitchen has a similarly vintage feel, with its wooden cabinets and butler's sink, although the kitchen units are actually from Ikea and have just been painted many times over. The simple wooden floorboards were laid by Tobit and painted grey, and the family eat at a well-worn round antique table from the eighteenth century. Lively artworks brighten up the walls, including a Chris Ofili print from the Serpentine Gallery and a picture of an African lady from an exhibition at the Hayward Gallery, as well as quirky drawings by friends, like Sophie Herxheimer's 'Nancy and the Lady in the Tree'.

Over the past twenty years, a small enclave of writers, photographers, artists and antiques dealers have made this unique corner of South London their home. Bloomsbury to Brixton might seem like a giant leap in lifestyle, but for Tobit, Nancy, and their neighbours, this shared artistic community is a wonderful reason to live here.

Detail of a velvet Georgina von Etzdorf throw and a cushion made from vintage fabric from Joss Graham.

The couple installed a wooden Ikea kitchen, which has since been repainted many times. An antique butler's sink and a Georgian table contribute to the vintage feel, while displayed on the wall is a drawing spelling 'Nancy' by the couple's friend Tony. Quirky finds fill the rest of the house, including a ceramic cow made by a member of the Bloomsbury group and inherited by Tobit from his father, Paul Roche.

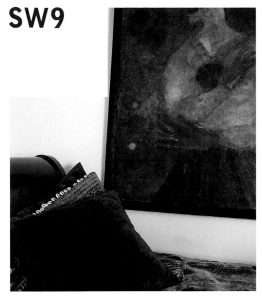

In the guestroom, an antique bateau-lit bed is covered with a velvet throw, and a cupboard is embellished with a favourite **YSL** handbag. A still life by **D**uncan Grant hangs above the fireplace, and bookshelves, paintings and stripey kilims fill the top-floor landing. Out back, the couple did not want a tidy urban garden, and opted for a wild green oasis instead, the perfect escape from the **B**rixton madness outside.

E1, E9, EC1, EC2
WHITECHAPEL
HACKNEY
CLERKENWELL
SHOREDITCH

An abundance of untouched historic warehouse buildings and elegant Georgian terraces, together with the area's close proximity to the City, have ensured that Whitechapel and Shoreditch have become two of the most expensive neighbourhoods in London. But despite its transformation over the past twenty years or so, Whitechapel still remains among the most deprived areas of Europe. The neighbourhood has historically been home to London's immigrants for hundreds of years: in the twentieth century alone, two hundred thousand Eastern European Jews were living in Whitechapel in 1914, while a new wave of immigrants arrived from Bangladesh and Pakistan in the 1950s.

A thriving French Protestant community of silkweavers lived and plied their trade in the Georgian terraces surrounding Spitalfields Market and Hawksmoor's Christ Church. Bomb-damaged and neglected, many of these houses had fallen into disrepair by the 1970s, and were painstakingly rebuilt by artists who came to live here in the decades following, such as Gilbert and George, who live in Fournier Street and frequent Les Trois Garçons (p. 130) in Club Row, off Bethnal Green Road, and Langlands + Bell (for this duo's house, see p. 138). Today, these historic houses count among the most desirable property to be found anywhere in the city. Artists have continued to live and work in the area, and the East End now boasts the highest concentration of artists in Europe, including Tracey Emin and Chris Ofili. The East End Jewish community also produced two of the twentieth century's most celebrated playwrights: Arnold Wesker, born in Stepney, and Harold Pinter, who was born in Hackney, where furniture designer Lisa Whatmough (p. 144) now resides.

LES TROIS GARÇONS
WHITECHAPEL

This converted Victorian pub now serves as the home, showroom and restaurant of three style mavens, and provides a focal point for the local artistic community in the heart of Whitechapel.

'Whitechapel has a different feel to it than any other part of London,' says Hassan Abdullah. 'There aren't any beautiful buildings or anything like that, but it's very happening.' Upon discovering a derelict pub in 1996, close to Brick Lane at the corner of Club Row and Bethnal Green Road, Hassan got together with two close friends, Michel Lasserre and Stefan Karlson, to buy the building. Its Grade II-listed status meant that the property had remained untouched until the three men moved in together to live and work in this unique space. Over the years, 'Les Trois Garçons' have become friendly with most of the residents of the surrounding streets, and they love the relaxed neighbourhood atmosphere of the area.

The pub was eventually converted into a home with a dining room on the ground floor, living space on the first floor, and bedrooms and bathrooms on the top floor. 'We hardly used our dining room,' recalls Hassan, 'so we thought we'd make it into a restaurant and see what happened.' An interior designer by trade, Hassan set about transforming the space in his signature baroque style, introducing a lavish, glamorous feel to the gritty East End. Suspended from the dining-room ceiling are antique chandeliers and delicate vintage handbags, while around the dimly lit room diners might glimpse a giraffe draped with necklaces, a stuffed tiger or swan, or a dramatic oil painting against the dark panelled walls. Artists, designers and architects who live locally have become frequent guests at the restaurant, with Gilbert and George coming for dinner every fortnight and Tracey Emin and Damien Hirst regularly holding court.

Hassan chose to treat the walls of the building as a neutral backdrop to his extraordinary collection of furniture and antiques, mostly supplied by dealers in France, Sweden and Italy who are familiar with his taste and keep things aside that he might like. In the sitting room alone there are five different shades of white, each chosen specifically to highlight the ceiling, cornicing and wood-panelling. Elements of colour are introduced through different compositions around the house, such as a display of vintage dresses along the bedroom corridor, or a stylish collection on the hallway landing featuring an English Regency chair, a dressmaker's dummy, and a pair of Christian Louboutin shoes.

Hassan deliberately chose to have a different look and feel in each of the rooms, from the cool grey bedroom to the granite-lined bathroom, carefully balancing contrasting colours and textures. The grey bedroom has a French bed decorated with the monogram of Marie Antoinette, together with an English nineteenth-century gold mirror for a hit of colour. Michel and Hassan's bedroom is painted midnight blue, with natural oak floors as a counterbalance. 'At night we dim the lights really low,' says Hassan, 'and it becomes a very comforting space.' Wanting to achieve the right balance of gold and blue, Hassan chose a sunburst theme, echoed in the golden rays behind the bed and in a rug by Verner Panton.

'Furniture has to be super modern-looking or old,' explains Hassan. 'I go for one or the other.' He particularly likes pieces from the 1940s to the 1970s, which he arranges next to eighteenth-century furniture to provide contrast and to focus the eye. The sitting room is an open-plan space occupying the whole of the first floor. Filled with sculptures, vintage chairs and sofas and hung with chandeliers, it looks like a beautiful and eclectic salon. It is a mix-and-match approach, with carefully chosen antiques ('which have a certain sense of romance and elegance') placed next to quirky modern pieces. When picking out the huge chandeliers and shimmering crystals that light up the room, Hassan insisted that they had to be unusual and original, such as the crystal galleon on top of a 1940s mirrored table, decorated with beads and ormolu by House of Baguettes. Around the room are marble busts and bronze sculptures by Mathurin Moreau, while in the brightly coloured annex next door hangs a lamp from the 1950s that was originally made for a Swiss bank.

In 1996, Whitechapel was still a no-go area for many of the trio's Chelsea and Notting Hill friends, but its rapidly changing urban environment and reputation as a stylishly cool destination has ensured that those friends are now all clamouring to move here. Over the next few years, the new East London Line and much-needed green space will be developed in this exciting, multi-ethnic and historic neighbourhood.

Detail of an Italian lamp from the 1960s, with coloured glass shades.

A 1950s lamp, one of sixteen originally made for a Swiss bank, makes a strong design statement in the colourful annex next to the sitting room; the round coffee table is a vintage piece from the 1970s. The dressing room takes its inspiration from gentlemen's outfitters, while in the luxurious bathroom, bold slabs of granite have been used to create dramatic flooring and as a foil to the Alessi fittings.

The neutral backdrop of the sitting room was created using five different shades of Farrow & Ball paint; the parquet flooring was salvaged from a town hall in Sweden. In this room, old and new sit comfortably together, such as the chaise longue by Nick Gough and an antique bust from France, and a birdcage (complete with parrot) placed next to a 1971 'Bulle' chair by Christian Daninos.

Natural oak floors provide a counterbalance to the midnight blue of the walls in Michel and Hassan's bedroom, while a golden sunburst – originally made for an Italian church in the seventeenth century – behind the bed and a rug by Verner Panton are in keeping with the blue-and-gold theme. A hand-made bedcover picked up by Michel from a souk in Damascus completes the look.

E1

LANGLANDS + BELL
WHITECHAPEL

Two artists have created a unique space in which to live and work out of an historic, bomb-damaged Georgian house – a former tailor's home – in the bustling East End.

Ben Langlands and Nikki Bell met at art college in the 1970s and first exhibited together as Langlands + Bell for their final degree show. Having exhibited internationally since the early 1980s, the duo were nominated for the Turner Prize in 2004, in recognition of work that ranges from interactive videos, such as the 'House of Osama Bin Laden', to installations depicting worldwide flight plans and monochromatic architectural ground plans. The changing architecture of Whitechapel, which has been their home for the past thirty years, continues to inspire their work.

Whitechapel remains a source of fascination to Ben and Nikki because of its heritage as a place that people have always flocked to – immigrants from different cultures have always found a home here. The couple also had a more pragmatic reason to move here: it was one of London's poorest boroughs and was a good place to find affordable accommodation that was still central. Over the years, Ben and Nikki have seen the face of the neighbourhood change as kosher restaurants and synagogues have closed down and been replaced with Bengali and Pakistani eateries and mosques. In the past, the shops and restaurants in the area traditionally shut down on Saturdays, before the Brick Lane and Spitalfields markets opened on Sundays. 'It used to be very quiet on a Saturday because of the Jewish Sabbath,' recalls Ben, 'but on Sundays it would all come alive again.'

Creatives such as broadcaster and historian Dan Cruikshank and artists Gilbert and George began to move here in the 1970s and 1980s, drawn by the cheap Georgian and early Victorian houses. 'There was a pioneering spirit,' remembers Nikki, 'with people discovering beautiful panelling inside their building and really appreciating what they had.' Everyone used to gather at the old Market Café, run by brother and sister Phyllis and Clyde Till, which became a pivotal meeting point where friendships were formed and neighbours would compare notes on each other's houses. By chance, Ben and Nikki even met the previous occupant of their own home, David Gould, who had moved out when a bomb dropped next door in 1942 and the house became unsafe to live in.

The building had been propped up with steel bars ever since, and repairing the bomb damage had to be Ben and Nikki's first priority. They employed specialist builders to repair the crack in the front wall of the house and to rebuild the roof, but decided to do the rest of the building work themselves, installing everything from plumbing and electricals to joinery and cupboards, which took a year of hard work. Layers of paint were stripped back from the wooden panelling in every room of the house, and the wooden floors were patched up and repaired. There is a history of people in the rag trade living here, including David Gould's family, who worked in the house as tailors. The top-floor room would originally have been the workshop, and the attic window had been installed to provide more light. This attic room is now Ben and Nikki's bedroom and bathroom, but they have kept a wooden tailor's stool here as a reminder of the room's former use.

The couple's approach to design has been influenced by their many trips to Japan. 'There are inherent things that we admire – the simplicity and notion of beauty, both inside and outside, and how you can combine those things,' Nikki explains. Having the minimum amount of furniture and belongings has great appeal to Ben. 'We don't really have much furniture and we like to keep it as simple as possible.' The low sofa and lacquered storage boxes in the sitting room were inspired by Japanese design, while the round table and chairs were chosen for their Georgian simplicity. Rather than buying a new dining table and chairs, they went out into the streets and came back with some wooden chairs that had been thrown out of a Hackney café, and metal table frames. Sculptures and found objects are stored in the 'clean studio' on the second floor, which relates to Ben and Nikki's first experiences of the East End and the history of the area. The couple have built tables and chairs with glass display boxes to hold the ephemera of everyday life. Ben wanted to 'reveal how the lives of ordinary people are also important and demand greater scrutiny.'

Living amongst the derelict and abandoned buildings of the East End and coming across abandoned Qur'ans, discarded toothbrushes, and even taxidermy was a formative experience for Ben and Nikki. Walking out their doorstep now, they are faced with velvet ropes in front of the city's most celebrated Indian restaurant and the looming skyline of the City of London, with its recently constructed skyscrapers. One of London's poorest boroughs is finally booming.

The duo made a series of work about Whitechapel, including this glass chair seat containing discarded toothbrushes, to highlight the transient lives of the local community.

The basement previously served as the sculpture studio, and still has the original concrete floor. The dining chairs had been thrown out into the street by a local café and were covered in grease, but have since been cleaned, varnished and recovered to create stylish seating. The curved plywood bathroom with its glass skylight was designed by a young **Ashley Hicks** when he was still an architecture student.

On the ground floor, a Georgian table, chairs and cast-iron range sit comfortably with lamps from the 1930s and '40s, reclaimed from a since-demolished dress-hire shop in the Whitechapel Road. Ben and Nikki found a consulting couch that had been discarded by the London Hospital, and chopped the legs off to create low-level seating. A row of neatly polished black shoes is lined up underneath.

LISA WHATMOUGH
HACKNEY

A stylish homeowner's own funky, fabric-wrapped designs lend flair and colour to this house in the East London borough of Hackney.

Lisa Whatmough's idiosyncratic designs utilize scraps of both new and vintage fabric to 'wrap' or reupholster antique furniture in a range of vibrant colours and styles. Lisa's work is keenly sought after by design stalwarts such as Liberty, who recognize that she has found a way to make old furniture look fresh and desirable again. Lisa trained as a sculptor and worked for an antiques dealer before opening up her own bespoke furniture and upholstery shop, Squint, in Redchurch Street near Spitalfields Market in 2005. Such is the success of her designs that she is planning to move to larger studio premises and open a new retail space in the coming year.

Because Lisa was keen to live and work in the same neighbourhood, she decided to trade in her flat with its roof terrace in Crouch End for a house with a garden in Hackney. She fell in love with only the second house she saw, despite the fact that the area was 'just about as grim as it could be', and bought it in 2004. At the time, she was just getting her first collection ready for Liberty and every room in the house had to be used for storage. But once Squint was open for business, Lisa was able to have a separate workroom in which to put together her designs and store fabric and furniture. For her own home, she wanted to create a tranquil environment in which to display her work, with soft grey walls and off-white eggshell floorboards creating a neutral backdrop.

There is a subtle difference between the furniture Lisa collects for her designs and the antique pieces that she selects for her home. She loves French antiques, but feels that they can often be too fussy and ornate to be further embellished with colourful textiles and embroidery. Instead, she often chooses to work with English or Irish Victorian furniture, in strong, plain shapes, which can be enhanced, rather than overwhelmed, by the additional decoration. For her own bedroom, she wanted pieces that were simple and elegant. 'It's not a very big bedroom,' Lisa explained, 'so it couldn't take anything too overpowering.' She picked out a black-and-gold Napoleonic-style French bed and an elegant dark wooden Arts and Crafts chair. The guest-room has an ornate carved mahogany bed, also French, but Lisa advises caution with this piece: 'You only need a little mahogany, as these pieces can be very heavy to live with and they can often suck all of the light of a room.'

In an ideal world, she would have more space around the bed to really show it off. She also took the opportunity to indulge in a more girly look to this room, with a 'wrapped' hanging rail and clothes hangers in floral fabrics and a bright-pink quilt with a gold-threaded trim.

Lisa is aware that her life is currently very work-focused, and, to balance this out, believes that it is essential to come home to a relaxed, calm space. She explains that the reason she works so hard is because she loves it, and she enjoys being surrounded by favourite pieces, many of which are her own designs that she can't bear to part with. The sitting room was designed to be a cosy and intimate space, and Lisa likes to come home and relax here on the reupholstered patchwork day bed. Although her friends find it irritating not to be able to sit on a sofa, this day bed is one of her favourite places to read, relax, and watch television. She stresses that a home is not just about surrounding yourself with functional pieces, it's also about collecting things because they're unusual or because, for some reason, you have an emotional connection to them. The room is filled with quirky pieces, from the wrapped candlesticks to the life-sized bust bought at auction and the antique shaving mirror.

The front room was meant to be entirely white, with white walls and floorboards, one of her own white paintings, and a piece of white lace over the window. Eventually, Lisa relented and allowed in some colour, in the form of 1960s lamp in swirly fabric from the King's Road, a 'wrapped' mirror to her own design, and a chair 'covered in various silks and quilted pieces'. This room is also used as an informal dining room, with vintage wooden benches and a table from the now-defunct furniture showroom Plinth, where she used to work. The downstairs kitchen has units made from 1960s filing cabinets, and a comfy 1920s chair, recovered with a funky fabric that is also from the 1960s.

Lisa currently shares her house with a beagle called Stan, but hopes that at some point she will able to invest in a bolthole in the countryside to provide them both with more outside space and an escape from busy urban life. She's already started to collect furniture for her country house: 'Sometimes you come across things which might not be quite right for this point in your life, but they are too difficult to walk away from.'

The frame surrounding an antique painting of the Virgin and Child has been has been given a fresh and updated look.

In the dining room, Lisa initially wanted to keep everything white, but couldn't resist introducing a few decorative elements, including the antique table and benches from Plinth and a 1960s lamp from Ena Green, a former antiques dealer in the King's Road. The wrapped teapot is Lisa's own design. Even Stan the beagle's favourite spot for an afternoon nap has received the Whatmough touch.

A French bed from the 1870s adds a bit of luxe to the guest bedroom, and Lisa likes the contrast between the antique bed and the white 1960s-style chest of drawers from Heal's. In the sitting room, a reproduction painting of Elizabeth I hangs on walls painted with 'Down Pipe' from Farrow & Ball. The floors are painted with white eggshell, to create a deliberately chipped, distressed look.

DAISY DE VILLENEUVE
CLERKENWELL

A stylish singleton's two-room basement flat in Clerkenwell is enhanced by vintage finds and family treasures, and doesn't skimp on colour and design.

The daughter of 1960s fashion photographer and style icon Justin and model Jan de Villeneuve, and sister of Poppy, also a photographer, illustrator Daisy de Villeneuve's artistic pedigree is well known. Having studied at Parsons School of Design in both Paris and New York, switching from a degree in fashion when she realized that she loved sketching and drawing to study fine art, Daisy is still the quintessential London girl at heart, equally at home in baggy jeans and battered Converse trainers as she is wearing a glamorous Missoni dress to the latest art opening. Her work is regularly in demand by *Vogue* and TopShop, for whom she designed a homeware range in 2004, and she recently turned her talents to designing a series of Moët & Chandon magnum bottles for the stylish Parisian store, Colette. At the moment, Daisy's home and studio are located in the basement flat of an eighteenth-century townhouse in Clerkenwell.

Keen to be at the centre of things, Daisy used to live in the heart of Notting Hill — Ladbroke Grove and Portobello Road – but was later tempted by a white-painted loft space in Clapham's Lavender Hill, in South London, where she lived for three years before settling in Clerkenwell in the summer of 2006. Her requirements for her new home were to live somewhere central, but also to find 'a place that looked pretty from the outside!' When she came across a sunny Georgian square in the centre of Clerkenwell, it was exactly what she had been looking for. As her new home only came with a bed and two kitchen stools, Daisy had to work hard to liven up this basement flat. Looking around her new place, Daisy remarks: 'Pretty much all of my things are vintage pieces, and I think that something too new or contemporary would just look odd. When I lived in Portobello Road, I would go to the market a lot, but I think that got it out of my system.' Her new hangout is now Exmouth Market in Clerkenwell, where she meets up with friends who live and work locally at Bar Kick, which suits her style perfectly and even has Italian flags painted on the floor.

Books and records have remained a constant in her life, and she has built up an extensive collection since her time at art school.

She inherited the LPs from her father, who was a music producer in the 1960s and '70s, and started to build up her own collection of '80s records from the Retro Music Exchange, in Notting Hill, an exchange shop where she can take in her old clothes and swap them for vintage records. Word has got out about Daisy's record collection, and she is often asked to DJ at parties – although she admits to not being particularly good! Her most treasured possessions are arranged on a shelf beside her bed: a punk-inspired photographic portrait by her father; an orange trinket box from Paris; and a book about Mulberry Street, a reminder of her old home in New York.

Living in a two-room flat with just a small bathroom, Daisy has to be resourceful and creative with her space. The sitting room has a desk, a sofa and an eat-in kitchen, while the bedroom has piles of books and records alongside the bed and a small cupboard for her clothes. Despite the lack of space, Daisy's flamboyant and colourful style is seen in such pieces as the sitting-room sofa, which is covered with a leopard-print throw from Biba, the cult London store that occupied the old Derry & Tom's building (now home to Whole Foods) in Kensington during the 1970s, and piles of African print cushions. Daisy draws all of her illustrations by hand at the 1950s desk, which is illuminated by a lamp from the 1940s, before scanning them into her computer to clean them up. She has a big pot of multi-coloured felt-tip pens to hand, but also works on delicate black and white images. Propped up next to the computer is a 'Babe Rainbow' picture by Sir Peter Blake, the artist behind The Beatles' legendary *Sgt. Pepper's Lonely Hearts Club Band* album cover and a family friend. At the opposite end of the sitting room, the bright-green kitchen area is full of vintage pieces, such as old tin plates and quirky teapots, along with Daisy's favourite sign, an old advertisement which reads 'Keep Active Hands Attractive Hands!' Her tiny bedroom has been livened up with a patchwork bedcover from Harbour Springs, in Michigan, and white vintage pillowcases from a friend in South Dakota.

Daisy's sharply drawn felt-tip marker portraits reveal the trials and tribulations of being a contemporary single thirty-something female living in London, and snatched fragments of conversations overheard on the bus or gossip at a Fashion Week party could end up as a witty one-liner in one of her limited-edition books, such as *He Said, She Said* and *I Told You So*. This small but stylish flat reflects the growing trend of many Londoners to live alone and to lead an independent, creative life.

Daisy's popular 'hand' drawings have been exhibited at Browns Focus, in London's South Molton Street.

Favourite pieces in the kitchen include a rug from the **Designers Guild** and a bread bin and teapot from **Portobello Road Market**. **Daisy** picked up her desk from **Squires Antiques** in **Faversham**, **Kent**, near her mother's house. **Displayed on the desk is an artwork by family friend Sir Peter Blake and a green lamp from CSAO**, in the **Marais** neighbourhood of **Paris**, all overlooked by **Daisy**'s own drawings.

The sitting-room sofa is covered with a leopard-print throw from Biba and a stack of African-print cushions. A suitcase from Globe-Trotter is used for additional storage. Favourite designs on business cards and mementoes from restaurants take pride of place, as does Daisy's recent publication *I Told You So*. The artist's essential felt-tip markers are stored close at hand in a vintage mug.

155

EC2

EMILY CHALMERS
SHOREDITCH

A former mini-cab office in a tiny Shoreditch street has been transformed into an airy, light-filled space on the edge of the City.

'I'm really particular about a lot of things, and incredibly particular about where I live,' admits interiors stylist Emily Chalmers. 'I'd rather be in our old Citröen van or camping out in a tent than in a flat that I didn't like.' After meeting at the Glastonbury Festival, Emily and her soon-to-be husband Chris moved down to London to share a flat in Hackney. Their landlord told them about another property they might be interested in: a ground-floor space in an old warehouse that had been used as a mini-cab office, tucked between the City and Spitalfields Market.

Emily had only seen the mini-cab office from the outside, and because she was out of the country on a work trip, had to trust Chris's opinion on the interior before they moved in. The street in which the warehouse was located dates back to the seventeenth century and was named after the inn that originally stood there, whose original buildings have long since vanished. Emily and Chris decided to take a chance on the open-place space, and moved into the building in April 2002, one month before they got married. The warehouse only had a tiny kitchen, a fairly basic bathroom and no heating, but it was exactly what they had been looking for: a blank canvas on which to make their mark. It was also just around the corner from Spitalfields Market, where Chris rented studio space for his work as a video director.

With its huge double doors, the warehouse is the perfect place for Emily to store sofas, chairs and tables for shoots. There are no storage cupboards, as Emily thought it would ruin the space's proportions, and she prefers to store her props and belongings on shelves. When friends came round to visit, they often thought it looked a bit like a shop because everything was out on view. The windows' deep ledges are used to display books, lamps and vases, and Emily is reluctant to put up blinds or curtains as she doesn't mind waking up with the sun. She hadn't originally intended to have a shop, but living in this space and collecting vintage furniture and objects inspired her to open her own interiors store, called Caravan, in 2005.

Dividing up a vast warehouse building into living areas relies on finding key pieces of bold furniture to make a big impact. Chris found a 1970s bed with a velour headrest and sides that would have overwhelmed any other bedroom, but which could make a statement here. Emily further defined the space by hanging green tropical-print drapes from the ceiling to create a modern four-poster. When Chris and Emily went to stay with her brother in Amsterdam, they found an old hunting table that was narrow and lightweight, and decided to ship it back to London. It arrived just in time for Christmas, and Emily managed to buy some wooden chairs from a café on Brick Lane and ran up a pile of brightly printed cushion covers to make the room look more colourful. With everything in place, the couple were able to invite fourteen people round for Christmas lunch. Alongside the dining table is an antique wooden roll-top desk, which used to belong to Chris, but has since been appropriated by Emily to use as her workspace. It is now surrounded with flowers, feathers and fabric, either displayed on the walls or neatly folded away.

Two large sofas define the living area: a Guy Rogers sofa that Emily picked up in Brixton for £20 and an old Chesterfield sofa. The Chesterfield was originally bought for Caravan, but she realized it was nicer than anything she had at home and decided to keep it! The wooden side-table with a circular opening holds all of Emily's hand-made sketchbooks from art college, and placed on top is one of Emily's favourite pieces: a sculptural lamp with a tall triangular shade. On the far wall Emily has hung a big round mirror, also found in Brixton, which she feels really helps to open out the space. And to make the whole area feel more cosy, Emily placed a cowhide rug on the floor, along with two gold leather bean bags. Separated from the main living space by a 1960s beaded curtain is a compact kitchen. In its mini-cab-office days, the kitchen had been very minimally furnished, but Emily found that she now needed lots of storage space for all of the bits and pieces that she uses for shoots. 'I've used every inch of space,' she explains, 'with hanging baskets from the ceiling, and things stored on top of the cupboards.'

Chris and Emily have possibly the easiest daily commute imaginable, as they can just stroll around the corner together to Spitalfields Market. Despite living in the centre of London, there is a great neighbourhood community, as most of the creatives working in Shoreditch also tend to live locally. The couple love the juxtaposition of the homey neighbourhood and markets, built up in the shadow of the skyline of the City of London.

Vintage chairs customized by Emily await weary guests.

Emily ran up the cushions for the dining chairs by using colourful fabric picked up at a French market. Favourite clothes and vintage pieces are displayed against the white-painted brick walls, as is essential haberdashery that is used as props on Emily's styling jobs. Ted the tabby, a rescue cat from the Battersea Dogs Home, thinks the textile-covered Chesterfield is a good place for a snooze.

A round mirror from Brixton Market, topped with a flower lamp by Helena Christensen for Habitat, hangs alongside a favourite vintage dress, together with an artwork that describes the couple's favourite things. Underneath it is an orange Anglepoise lamp from a flea market. The large artwork against the wall is called 'Bunny Boy' and is by Brooklyn-based artist collective, Faile.

A view to the main living space, glimpsed through a lace curtain that separates it from the kitchen. The bed, just seen behind the sofa, is screened behind drapes made by Emily. She prefers to have favourite clothes and shoes out on display, rather than hidden away in bulky wardrobes that would take up too much space. On sunny mornings, Emily takes her coffee out into the courtyard.

Royal Borough

and Chelsea

W1, W2, W8, W10, W11

MARYLEBONE

BAYSWATER

KENSINGTON

NORTH KENSINGTON

NOTTING HILL

In the early eighteenth century, London's West End was developed into the four neighbourhoods of Fitzrovia, Marylebone, Mayfair and Soho. Then as now, the city's wealthiest and most influential residents chose to live in Mayfair. By the nineteenth century, the small village of Marylebone had also become a fashionable residential area – Victorian writers like Dickens, George Eliot and Wilkie Collins made their home here, while in *Vanity Fair* Thackeray described nearby Portman Square as one of London's most desirable addresses – and today is home to the likes of Madonna and Guy Ritchie.

Just on the other side of the Edgware Road is Bayswater, known for its large Greek and Arab communities (the latter clustered around the Edgware Road), and for its busy thoroughfares of Queensway and Westbourne Grove, anchored by Whiteleys, London's first department store and now a retail and cinema complex. Further west still is the affluent neighbourhood of Kensington (which together with Chelsea forms London's only 'royal' borough), bisected by Kensington High Street, recently named as London's second-best shopping street. North Kensington forms the northernmost tip of Notting Hill, defined by the main arteries of Ladbroke Grove and Golborne Road.

Notting Hill itself is one of London's most stylish and sought-after neighbourhoods, with a heady mix of actors, supermodels and fashion designers based here, including Sienna Miller and Stella McCartney. Despite its glamorous reputation, it was home to some of the worst slums in London, the 'Piggeries and Potteries', throughout the nineteenth century and was notorious for its unscrupulous landlords in the twentieth. It was only when Notting Hill became a conservation area in 1967 that the Victorian terraces and villas were restored and rebuilt, and the neighbourhood became a desirable place to live.

ADAM HILLS + MARIA SPEAKE
MARYLEBONE

A glass penthouse, designed by the owner's father, atop an Edwardian mansion block in Marylebone makes the transition from party pad to family home with ease.

When two young architecture students from Glasgow University moved down to London in 1997 to launch their architectural salvage business Retrouvius, they thought they had landed the ultimate party pad when they took up residence in a glass penthouse in Marylebone. Eleven years later, Adam Hills and Maria Speake have two small children and their needs have completely changed. Rather than throwing rooftop parties, they found themselves needing to make the entire place more baby-friendly.

The penthouse was designed and built in 1973 by Adam's father, the architect Nicholas Hills, who attached a new glass building onto an Edwardian mansion block. He used the exterior walls to form the structure of the bedrooms and bathroom: the turret became a round bedroom and the dormer windows formed part of the smaller bedroom and a bathroom. Almost all of the flat is taken up with generous shared living areas, with only a minimal amount of space has been put aside for the bedrooms.

Very little work had been done to the apartment since it was first built, but Maria was keen to smarten up the place before the arrival of their new baby. Given the nature of their business, the couple wanted to use as many reclaimed materials as possible, such as the big marble slabs for the kitchen worktop that came from Blagdens fishmonger in Marylebone. Maria loved the little channels carved into the marble, but to her dismay the stonemason decided to polish up the marble and remove any 'imperfections'. To echo the use of aluminium on the cruciform columns and around the window glazing, Maria used sheet aluminium on the doors of the kitchen units, while a 1950s lamp with coloured shades (a salvage find that Maria persuaded Adam to keep for the house rather than selling on) is suspended above the worktop.

The kitchen was originally located in the centre of the flat. A logical choice at the time, it has since proved to be too small a space, especially with all of the couple's friends crowding in. 'We weren't using the space properly,' Maria remembers, 'and everyone spent all of their time in the kitchen.' With such a young family, she really wanted to have a much larger eat-in kitchen, and decided to create one out of her old studio/office, converting the old kitchen into a new study and workspace. Adam and Maria used reclaimed laboratory countertops to make the rest of the kitchen units, and Maria loves the smooth grain and warmth of this polished wood. Among Adam's more unusual salvage pieces were the various old London Underground signs that were being replaced. The Northern Line sign has now become their kitchen table, after Adam turned it on its side and added salvaged wood for legs. Pulled up to the table are BA 21B chairs designed by Ernest Race, complementing the graphic statement of the Underground sign with their white aluminium frames and cherry-red upholstery.

The distinctive diagonal print used for the carpets, curtains and tiles was designed by Nicholas Hills and is the signature theme throughout the flat. It was important to Maria that they respected the integrity of her father-in-law's designs, so when the original blinds needed replacing, she picked out a vintage hand-painted fabric and used it on the diagonal to make new ones. In the sitting room, the couple's main priority has been to clear most of the furniture out of the way so that the children can kick their footballs and run around. All that remains is a stove (which burns smokeless fuel), a wooden bench made from reclaimed poles, a fabric PK 22 chair by Paul Kjaerholm, and a white leather chair by Joseph Palumbo that Nicholas Hills bought for the flat when it was first built. As a concession to the couple's son Marcus, a wooden swing hangs from the ceiling. The sign on the back wall reads AVE MARIA, although when Adam found it in an antiques fair, he read it as AVH MARIA – his initials and her name! There is also a cosy window seat with fabric cushions by Nicholas Hills and Felix Spicer.

This Marylebone space has turned out to be the ultimate in flexible living, just as capable of accommodating fifty people for a party as coping with the demands of two small toddlers. Adam and Maria constantly move their furniture around the flat to meet their changing needs: a leather bench seat works just as well in the bathroom as it does in the sitting room as extra seating. Maria's greatest challenge is to hang on to her favourite items of furniture, before Adam can rush down to the warehouse with his latest find!

The couple's eldest son Marcus puts a wooden swing through its paces in front of a wooden bench that was designed by this parents, using poles removed from a demolition site in the City of London.

The marble worktop in the kitchen is a reclaimed piece from a local fishmonger; above it is a vintage lamp with coloured shades from the 1950s. The kitchen units on the far wall are made from recycled lab tops, while the table has been fashioned from a **London Underground** sign, with salvaged wooden legs added. The bathroom has remained virtually unchanged since 1973, set off by the signature graphic print.

In the corner turret, a round bed is covered with a vintage fur rug and a 'Love' cushion from **By Guru in Copenhagen**. Light is supplied by a vintage Anglepoise lamp, against an antique relief from **Retrouvius**, and a vintage fixture from the 1970s, which makes a striking contrast to the pleated fabric roof. The table is surrounded by **Ernest Race** chairs that have been upholstered in bright, cherry-red fabric.

W1

JANE COLLINS
MARYLEBONE

The Italian 1940s provide the inspiration for this Palladian-style house in Marylebone, and is a fitting backdrop to a collection of key vintage finds.

In the late 1990s, stylist Jane Collins felt that retail had become a little too safe and boring, so she decided to do something about it. Her boutique Sixty6, a mix of antique furniture and objets d'art and contemporary fashion, duly opened on Marylebone High Street in 1997. Jane's unique approach immediately appealed to the street's well-heeled shoppers, who were looking for something on the quirky side, rather than just the usual little black dress.

For her own home, Jane and her husband Stephen had found a white stucco Palladian-style house near Marylebone, some years earlier in 1988. 'We drastically changed the space,' remembers Jane. 'It used to look completely different, and was only a third of the size.' As their family grew with the arrival of a daughter and a son, the couple managed to buy the flat next door in 1994, and another adjoining flat ten years later. 'We started buying and collecting furniture and objects together when we first got married, on every holiday and every trip,' recalls Jane, 'and we still do.' Rather than settle for the usual wedding-list items from John Lewis like toasters and oven-gloves, the couple chose to cash in the money from their wedding and buy one perfect, wooden Biedermeier-style table from the 1930s: 'It was much more special to have one fabulous thing,' as Jane says.

The family like to spend most of their time in the open-plan sitting room on the ground floor, with its large conservatory that opens out into the garden. Jane chose to display modern pieces in this spacious room, such as the curved turquoise-and-chrome chairs from the 1970s, placed beneath a row of Italian stainless-steel lamps. She catches up on essential correspondence at a black-and-chrome 1930s Kassel desk, which holds a collection of Holmegaard glass vases from the 1960s and a favourite 1960s-style lamp with a Perspex base. A dining area is screened off from the main space for more formal dining, but family meals tend to take place around the white Arne Jacobsen table in the kitchen.

Jane's love of the style of the Italian 1940s can be seen in the double-height seating area on the first floor, which boasts curvy sofas, armchairs and side-tables from the period, all with elegantly tapered legs. Groups of glass vases are displayed around the room, from 1940s Italian glass to Scandinavian pieces from the 1960s. Jane's favourite objects are the tiny sculptures by Franz Hagenauer that date to the 1930s: 'I'm very sentimental about those as they were given to me by my husband,' Jane says. She also designed a cosy area in the upstairs gallery, complete with slouchy sofas piled high with Ralph Lauren cashmere cushions, where the whole family can gather together to watch television.

The 1940s also caught Jane's imagination when it came to designing her bedroom, which she has furnished with gilt-and-crystal chandeliers, an antique dressing table, and a velvet armchair. This room is an exercise in contrasting textures, where a highly polished chest of drawers is placed next to shagreen bedside tables. Rather than choosing sensible neutral colours for the kitchen and bathrooms, Jane again wanted to do something a little out of the ordinary. 'We sprayed the kitchen pistachio green with a car-spray lacquer for a high-gloss sheen,' she recalls. Even the kitchen stools are a Charlotte Perriand design from the 1930s. Inspiration for the bathroom, too, came from the 1930s, specifically from a Cubic-style opaque pink glass bottle: 'It has an old-fashioned feel, like the bathroom of a pre-war mansion block or an old-world hotel,' Jane says.

Jane and Stephen's home is a testament to twenty-five years of collecting and creating a home together. Their Marylebone house is full of vintage finds, and the only new items are the fixtures and fittings in the kitchen and bathrooms. As more and more people have started to collect twentieth-century design, Jane has found it increasingly hard to find a bargain, but she admits that if she falls in love with a piece, she has to have it. 'I love buying and selling,' she admits, 'but I know I can't keep everything.

Stylish costume jewelry provides a sophisticated contrast to the muted colour palette used throughout the house.

The Biedermeier-style wooden table was made in the 1930s, while the wire chairs with their original canvas upholstery are 1940s French. In the conservatory, favourite vintage pieces such as Eero Saarinen's 'Tulip' table and chairs by Arne Jacobsen are on display. Jane's collection of 1940s Italian glass and Scandinavian pieces from the 1960s add colour and drama to the double-height sitting room.

The ornate cornicing of the ceiling makes for a bold statement in the Palladian-style sitting room, where Jane designed a cosy television nook with a slouchy sofa and Ralph Lauren cashmere cushions.

A chrome-and-black Kassel desk from the 1930s holds a collection of glass vases and a favourite lamp with a Perspex base, and is set off by a Pierre Cardin-esque wooden chair from the 1950s.

SIMON TEMPLETON
BAYSWATER

Behind the stately Georgian terrace of Connaught Square, a tiny mews house converted by its architect owner is now a study in sophisticated minimalism — and has a surprising new owner.

As a newly married couple in 2000, Simon and Gillian Templeton were looking for an affordable house in Central London when they came across this run-down 1820s mews cottage just behind Connaught Square. They managed to buy the property the following year (with sealed bids), but this was only the beginning of a process of restoration and labour of love that was to take around sixteen months to complete. Gillian placed a great deal of trust in her architect husband, as her first impression was that the mews resembled a student hovel and she was finding it difficult to imagine its future transformation into a stylish, contemporary home.

This little mews house would originally have been annexed to a main house, one of the Georgian terraced houses in Connaught Square that back onto the row of mews. In the nineteenth century, the cobblestone ground floor of the smaller house would have been home to two horses and a carriage, while the driver would have lived on the floor above. The mews basement connects through to the main house, and would originally have been used as a kitchen and scullery. Simon and Gillian first checked with their neighbours to make sure that the basement was unoccupied; in this posh part of London, it would not have been inconceivable to find a swimming pool or a snooker table lurking beneath their home. In clearing out the basement (the process took fifteen skips!), the couple were delighted to discover around 100 square metres of York stone, which Simon suspected was from the original basement floor of the Connaught Square house. The enormous brick arches, over two metres at their widest point and sandwiched together with bright-yellow, two-hundred-year-old sand, would originally have supported the weight of the horses and carriage overhead. This subterranean space is now completely unrecognizable, having been converted into a bedroom and a bathroom, together with a small study area, with a light well flooding the rooms with much-needed natural light.

Simon designed a solid oak spiral staircase with a glass handrail to unify the three floors, and used large floor tiles made from Sicilian marble (20cm thick) to increase the feeling of floor space, as well as installing underfloor heating in the basement and ground floor. Almost everything in the house is white, from the floors to the kitchen, and even the pair of classic Mies van der Rohe 'Barcelona' chairs and matching footstool, while the woodwork has a veneer of North American oak. The base for the dining table was adapted from a metal prototype for a Norman Foster 'Nomos' design, and is surrounded with contemporary chairs from Aria. Upstairs, Gillian wanted to bring a more boudoir-like feel to the master bedroom and dressing room. The bed is covered with an oyster-coloured satin quilt from Space Boudoir, and the floor with warm fur rugs. Favourite bags, shoes and evening dresses are left out on display in the dressing area, which is illuminated by a sinuous Art Déco lamp featuring a black-painted cat. Embroidered organza curtains and a grey carpet further soften the feel of these rooms.

Life in a mews house has been a unique experience, as Gillian explains: 'It is a community that looks out for each other, and I've never really experienced that in London before.' To create a sense of privacy, the couple planted three large olive trees in white-painted containers to screen their living area, and loved to sit outside here on a hot summer's evening, literally out on the street, surrounded by good friends and neighbours.

In 2004, the main house on Connaught Square was bought by former Prime Minister Tony Blair and his wife, Cherie, and when Simon and Gillian considered selling their own property in 2007, the Blairs quickly snapped it up. Impressed with the use of space and the design of the Templetons' home, the Blairs decided to employ Simon as their own architect. The brief was to completely refurbish the Connaught Square house and to find a way to link the two houses to create one unified space. The main terraced house now provides grand entertaining spaces, but the Blairs thought that the ground floor of Simon and Gillian's mews house would be ideal for a cosy family kitchen of their own.

A row of olive trees discreetly screens the front of Simon and Gillian's mews house in Bayswater.

The low grey sofa in the sitting room is from Capellini, and the 'Barcelona' chairs and ottoman are design classics by Mies van der Rohe; Simon designed the storage and lighting system on the far wall himself. In the dining room, the tabletop was also made by Simon, and is fitted onto a prototype base by Norman Foster. The dining chairs are stackable garden chairs from Aria, bought for £20 each.

In the upstairs bedroom, oyster-coloured satin bedlinen from Space Boudoir adds warmth and helps to soften the austere lines of the space. The neutral colour scheme in the sitting room is picked up by such details as sculptural white candles, a paper pleated vase and some shells displayed in a contemporary wooden bowl, while an Art Déco lamp in the shape of a cat illuminates Gillian's dressing room.

W8

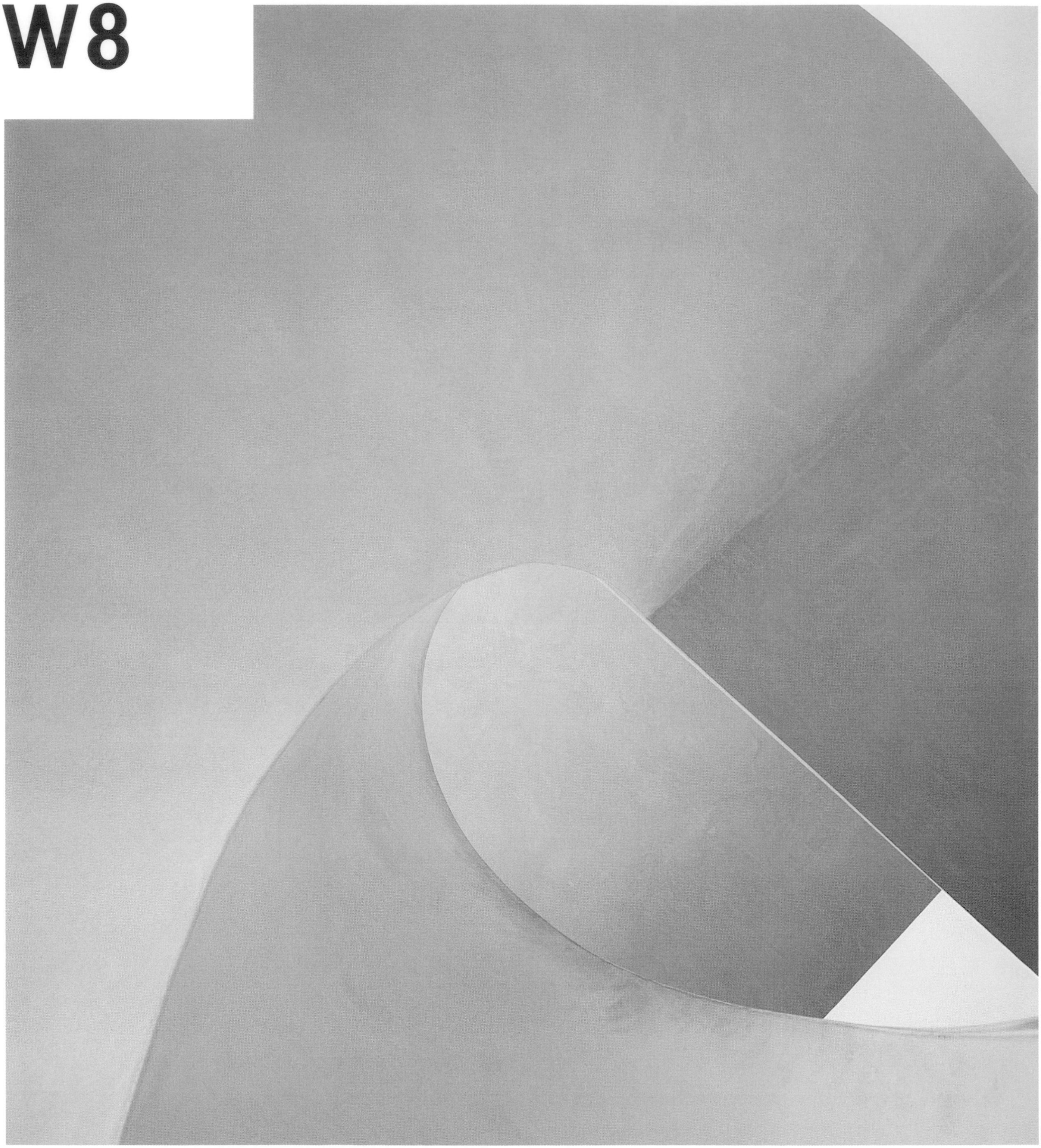

CAROLE CONRAD KENSINGTON

A 1960s apartment block designed by Richard Seifert on the world's most expensive street has been turned into a coolly minimalist interior with the help of architect David Chipperfield.

In 1996, with their children grown up and no longer living at home, Carole and Neville Conrad found themselves ready for a dramatic change in their lives. They decided to move out of their Victorian family house in Holland Park and into the top-floor flat of a starkly modern apartment building at the north end of the exclusive Kensington Palace Gardens, overlooking the embassy of the Czech Republic. The building's architect, Richard Seifert, had achieved recognition and some notoriety for such uncompromising buildings as the NatWest Tower in the City and the iconic Centrepoint building at the corner of Tottenham Court Road. Carole wanted to live 'in a more contemporary way, in a loft-type space', although her husband needed rather more convincing about the merits of open-plan living. No other buyers wanted to take on the bare shell, which had been completely stripped out by a developer, but Carole was undaunted by such a blank canvas. Work on the flat took just over two and a half years, and the couple finally moved into their new home in June 1999.

The Conrads chose to work with architect David Chipperfield, who is known for his sensitive approach to Modernist spaces, but Carole was anxious not to create anything too minimalist or austere: 'We wanted to keep it simple, but still get warmth and texture into the space.' The walls were finished with hand-polished plaster and were intended to display the couple's art collection, but when it came to hanging the paintings, Carole and Neville found they couldn't bear to touch the pristine expanses. As a result, there are no pictures anywhere in the house, and instead the couple decided to display their collection of contemporary ceramics, by such celebrated makers as Edmund de Waal, whose sculptural shapes seem to perfectly complement the design of the flat. 'The space seemed almost like a work of art itself, so I wanted to keep it pure,' Carole explains.

Carole and Chipperfield had a close working relationship, meeting up every two weeks to discuss the building's progress. Carole was a thorough client and keen to explain their lives, right down to the last detail of how many dresses, suits and pairs of shoes she and Neville had. 'Only you know how you want to live,' Carole observes. 'The architect can't get inside your mind, so you have to be very precise about what you want.' After a few months, Carole felt that Chipperfield instinctively understood the way that she and Neville wanted to function in their own home. Architect and client's shared perfectionist streak is revealed within the flat, as there are no grilles, radiators, pipes or electric points to be seen. Everything has been hidden away, and even the spotlights made from opaque glass are perfectly in line with the ceiling.

Chipperfield designed most of the furniture for the space, from the dining table and chairs to the folding metal tables and hand-woven green rugs. The curved screen and headboard in the bedroom are covered with abaca, a banana fabric from the Philippines. Within Carole's custom-made desk are the wires for the printer and computer, cleverly concealed within the legs and desktop; the bedside tables also conceal the controls for the lighting and music. The walk-in wardrobe is made from American black walnut, with separate cupboards for Carole's shoes and handbags and even pull-out shelves for her neatly rolled-up Issey Miyake pleated clothing. For the bathroom, Chipperfield wanted to insert an entire marble block into the space to create one integral unit. The result, made from alabaster travertine, forms a separate but free-standing unit between the bedroom and dressing room. The walls, floor, bath and sink are all made from marble from the same quarry, while heating pipes run beneath the bath to warm the marble and prevent the bath water from getting cold. Running along a mirrored wall is a long marble basin with a tap at each end, which Chipperfield considered less fussy than two sinks.

As the design progressed, elements of the building began to change, with the main staircase becoming more sculptural and the smaller staircase in the hallway reduced to a simpler design. The large staircase leads from the ground-floor living space up to the first-floor gallery, where Carole has placed her desk, with a curved screen behind it to conceal the bedroom area. She was keen to have her study in the centre of the flat, and enjoys using all 465 square metres of the space. The most striking aspect of the flat is the light flooding in through the double-height windows, filtered by the mature trees on either side of the building. The soft green colours are picked up inside with rugs by Chipperfield and cushions by Kate Blee. Neville is still to be convinced by open-plan living, but the couple agree that creating a custom-built home together has been a wonderful adventure.

A detail of the curved sculptural staircase that provides a link between the ground floor and the first floor of the flat.

Architect David Chipperfield and textile designer Kate Blee designed the sofas and soft furnishings to pick up on the muted green colours of nearby Kensington Gardens. In the bedroom, a curved screen made of abaca provides privacy; the bed's frame is made from the same material. A long shelf displays Carole and Neville's collection of contemporary ceramics by Edmund de Waal and Rupert Spira.

The bathroom floor and long basin are both made from alabaster travertine marble, while the large bathtub is made up of two solid pieces of marble fitted together. Pipes running beneath the floor keep the stone warm and prevent the bath from getting cold. In the bedroom, the doors of the bespoke wardrobes in American black walnut slide back to reveal drawers, shelving and hanging space.

JUSTIN THORNTON + THEA BREGAZZI
NORTH KENSINGTON

A modern design couple have created a fresh, funky and comfortable home in West London that is inspired by the past.

Justin Thornton and Thea Bregazzi, Isle of Man natives who met when they were teenagers, launched fashion label Preen in 1996. Their designs are now worn by the likes of Kate Moss, Chloë Sevigny and Amy Winehouse, with the menswear favoured by musicians such as Bobby Gillespie from Primal Scream and the lads from the Arctic Monkeys. The couple have always loved Portobello Market for its vintage clothes and antique furniture, and Thea couldn't imagine living and working anywhere else. They wanted to live within walking distance of their home and studio on Portobello Green, and bought this terraced Victorian house in 2005.

'We've always collected lots of bits and pieces,' explains Thea, 'and we like the contrast between new and old.' The sitting room perfectly illustrates this contrast between contemporary and vintage design, with its mirrored table, designed by the couple, surrounded by Victorian chairs stuffed with horsehair and antique wooden chairs that were originally intended for use in churches, complete with a storage section at the back for prayer books (these now hold Preen's look books). Framing the mantelpiece is a cluster of silver flowers that doubles up as a lamp, and a contemporary art piece made from hundreds of white balloons, designed to look at first glance like petals or shells. Justin and Thea particularly like this kind of three-dimensional trompe l'oeil, as seen in their white floor lamp with its round drum shade, which is made entirely from stainless steel.

The couple only made a few structural changes when they moved into their house, simply knocking down the wall between the living and dining areas to create a light, open-plan space. During the summer months, Justin and Thea spend most of their time here, with the double-doors opened out onto the garden. For the colder winter months, the couple wanted to make sure that they had working fireplaces and fashioned a snug on the first floor in front of one of them. To create a warm environment, the walls were painted in greeny-grey 'Pigeon' from Farrow & Ball, with one wall lined with a grid of bookshelves to hold their trade books. Inspired by one of their own recent collections that featured hot pink, the couple invested in an equally pink 'Egg' chair by Arne Jacobsen,

and made up cushions from scraps of fabric used in past collections. The floor lamp is a one-off piece made from casts of antique table legs, placed one on top of the other to create a unique porcelain stand. Shelves next to the fireplace hold a group of white Russian dolls designed by Martin Margiela; the reading lamp next to the leather armchair is called 'Miss Pac' and was designed by Alvin Bagni for Habitat to look like Pac Man.

Justin teases Thea that she was born wearing a Vivienne Westwood mini-crini; to prove his point, he dug out an old photograph of Thea in a red dress aged four, already the fashionista, and had it enlarged onto a canvas. Thea's even spent the past few years wearing Westwood's infamous high-heeled shoes, with their four-inch platform. 'I don't know how I did it!' she admits. 'They're gorgeous, but they are pretty precarious.' Thea's collection of contemporary and vintage fashion is stored upstairs in her dressing room, bedroom and walk-in wardrobe. One of her favourite pieces is a Victorian mourning jacket with jet beading: 'It's incredible the way the jacket is made and boned,' she says. 'You don't find things like this any more in the market.' The bedroom and bathroom both have an old-fashioned, romantic feel. For the bedroom, the couple chose contemporary textiles, including a satin quilt from Laura Ashley and embroidered cushions from cult fashion label Ghost. Favourite treasures, such as the stack of hand-bound Bibles and a collection of vintage butterflies, are displayed on the mantelpiece. In the bathroom, swathes of antique lace hanging from the window complement an antique armchair and French enamel jug.

Thea and Justin's love of antique clothing and furniture, with its intricate detailing and hand-embroidery, can be seen in their meticulous approach to their own collections. Given their body-con, slim-fitting designs, it would seem at first that Justin and Thea are the ultimate Modernists. In reality, this fashionable pair are constantly collecting and being inspired by the designs of the past.

In keeping with Justin and Thea's love of all things vintage, an acrylic '746 Series' telephone is displayed on a stack of fashion magazines.

A mirrored dining table designed by Justin and Thea is surrounded by 'DSW' dining chairs by Charles and Ray Eames and antique chairs, including some wooden ones from a church. A cluster of silver flowers doubles up as a lamp, above which is a contemporary artwork made from hundreds of white balloons. In the snug, a hot pink 'Egg' chair is a striking contrast to walls painted in 'Pigeon' from Farrow & Ball.

In the stylish bathroom, a window is hung with vintage lace and gold paper trim from India, while the porcelain sink and tongue-and-groove walls provide a sophisticated contrast to the shabby chic of the second-hand armchair. For a more modern look and to continue the distressed theme, Justin and Thea have chosen to leave the staircase unpainted, rather than putting down traditional carpet.

W10

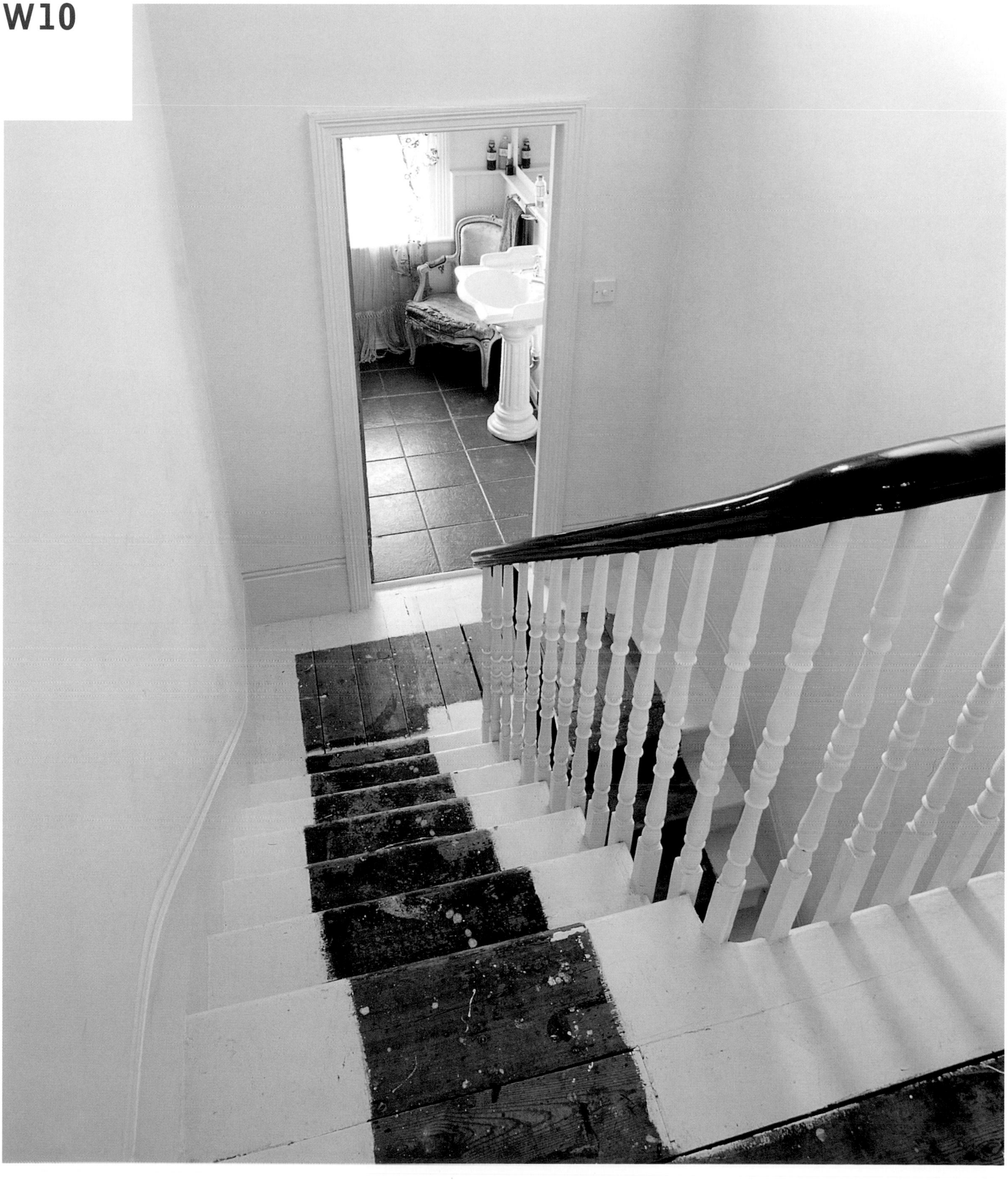

The framed butterfly case in the bedroom was a gift from friend and milliner Lucy Barlow, while a vintage leather armchair is just the right height for Monty the terrier to gaze out of the window. The sitting room is illuminated by a 'Spun' floor lamp designed by Sebastian Wrong for Flos. In the opposite corner, a TV sandwiched between a stack of magazines supports a gold-plated fruit bowl by Harry Allen.

W11

SAM ROBINSON
NOTTING HILL

The owner of an influential lifestyle boutique in Notting Hill brought the same eye for bold colour and unusual details when it came to designing her new home around the corner.

Having lived in West London all her life, Sam Robinson has a unique understanding of the area, from the local markets on Portobello Road to the quieter, more villagey neighbourhoods. She even knew the exact street that she wanted to live on, and waited patiently for a house to come on the market – which it did in 2004 – so that she could make an offer on the same day. Sam knows everyone in her street (perhaps uniquely for London), but this may be due to her unusual house-moving process, in which she simply enlisted friends and neighbours to carry her furniture and possessions down the street to the new house!

Sam already owned a business around the corner in Clarendon Cross with her partner Sarah O'Keefe, and loved the idea of being able to walk to work. When Sam and Sarah opened The Cross in 1996, it created an immediate sensation. Their shop quickly became a cult destination and gained a reputation for stocking quirky boho-chic designs and unashamedly girly fashions. Reflecting the interests of the twenty-something owners, vintage pictures were hung on the wall alongside glamorous party dresses and children's toys. A new housewares shop, Cross The Road, is located just opposite the original boutique.

Sam's husband Charlie Hall loves her sense of style, and encouraged his wife to exercise the same bold approach throughout their own home (although she does consult him before forging ahead with floral prints and textiles to make sure the overall effect isn't too pink). The couple wanted the ground floor to be one big open-plan living and dining area, with pale-green floorboards to contrast with the Samarkand rugs from Uzbekistan and translucent resin floor lamps from the Philippines. Sam chose a print from Timorous Beasties for the blinds, while the armchairs and sofa are covered with cushions and throws from The Cross and New York-based Dosa. Hanging on the wall is Gerald Laing's cult series 'Bikini Girls', which Sam found years ago in a junk shop. Sam's signature style might sound jarring, as she drapes fairy lights around a butterfly painting or turns Moroccan wedding throws into cushions, but somehow it all comes together. When it

came to designing the kitchen, Charlie was allowed free rein – which Sam thought was only fair as she can't cook. The couple love to entertain, so Sam stocked up on catering glasses as she realized that her own beautiful antique glasses weren't going to last long. The kitchen units are from Ikea, with work surfaces made from reclaimed school laboratory desks, and the fixtures and fittings are from Buyers and Sellers, in Ladbroke Grove. But Sam's influence can also be seen in the eclectic mix of new and vintage finds, including a Nigerian wedding pot.

Sam was able to indulge her girly side in the bedroom, however. She made a beeline to Celia Birtwell's shop (one of her favourite designers), picking out a subtle floral print for the blinds, and chose an antique quilt from Sheila Cook and had cushions made from her own collection of vintage textiles. On the landing is another classic Sam touch: an old, white-painted wooden chair upholstered with a Union Jack print, with a super-luxe needlepoint 'Jubilee' cushion, also in a Union Jack pattern, on top, designed by *Vogue* fashion director Lucinda Chambers for The Rug Company. The bathroom has a deliberately old-fashioned feel, with a roll-top bath and a vintage rose theme, echoed in the shelves from Miv Watts (actress Naomi's mother) and an antique mirror from Cath Kidston. Charlie's work, organizing cultural tours and visits for students in Venice, means that he spends several months of the year in Italy, and their sons' bedrooms are full of posters from Venice and drawings of gondolas to remind them of him. Each of the boys' beds has a hand embroidered cover made by Shirley McLauchlan, stitched with lines from nursery rhymes, together with images of their favourite things (including Lily the dog!).

Outside, Sam and Charlie designed a walled garden filled with palm trees, banana trees and bamboo plants. It's very much used as an outdoor room, with wooden decking and a courtyard cobbled with pebbles. Sam found some striped fabric to make huge floor cushions for the decking, and picked out a vivid sunshade from her own shop (every year, Sam designs a different garden collection for The Cross in her trademark stripes and prints). Just before Sam met Charlie, he had lost everything in a house fire, including an amazing collection of books and records. He had to start again with nothing, but Sam admits that in her he met someone 'who had way too much stuff, so it worked out perfectly.' Charlie is building up a new record collection, but has also embraced Sam's style with enthusiasm, and plenty of pink cushions, vintage textiles and paintings have found their way into his garden shed.

A bed is covered with a vintage quilt from Sheila Cook and a cushion made to Sam's design using antique textiles.

In the sitting room, a round resin lamp from the Philippines is balanced on a pouf from **Dosa**, while floor cushions from **The Cross** provide a comfortable and colourful spot for Lily the dog to have a snooze. An armchair from **Myriad** is covered with a throw from **The Cross** and tie-dyed **Dosa** cushions, while displayed against the wall is a butterfly picture by **Chris Kenny**, above a screen from **Miv Watts**.

The bathroom's vintage rose theme is played out in the wooden shelving from **Miv Watts** and paintings from **Wild at Heart**. A rose chandelier from **Tuchra** in **Fulham**, which specializes in antiques from Damascus, is a dramatic addition to Sam's bedroom. In the dining room, one of Sam's favourite pieces, a painting by **Rebecca Miller-Cheevers**, hangs above a table from **Bazar** in the **Golborne Road**.

A Paul Smith shirt makes for an alternative artwork above Sam's bed. The children's beds and rocking horse were found in a junk shop, while the curtains are from Cath Kidston and the cowhide rug is from Made. In Charlie's garden shed, a Chesterfield sofa is piled with cushions from Megan Park, and on the side table is a lamp by the couple's friend Martha Krempel (p. 52), with a fabric shade in 'Woods'.

CARINA COOPER
NOTTING HILL

French dairies and boudoirs of the 1930s and '40s are the inspirations behind this coolly sophisticated Arts and Crafts family home in Notting Hill.

Cookery writer Carina Cooper likes to use the best organic produce in her own cooking, and fortunately for her, her local neighbourhood of Notting Hill has the pick of food markets, delis and specialist shops. Inspired by the area's Spanish, Portuguese and West Indian communities, she will often create new dishes with fresh ingredients, or update an old classic.

Carina found her home in 2006 by walking around the neighbourhood, familiarizing herself with favourite streets and houses, until one quirky Arts and Crafts house caught her eye. She discovered through a local estate agent that it had been on the market for eighteen months, almost unheard of in Notting Hill. The layout felt a little dated as the same family had lived here for forty years; there was a central staircase with parlours leading off it, but no big rooms that could be converted into a sitting room or a large kitchen. Carina was really looking for a large family home for herself and her four daughters, who are home-schooled, and tried to work out if there was a way to open out the rooms, or to extend the house to create more space. In the end, she decided to make an offer and to build a two-storey extension, which would extend out into the garden, and create a 24-foot kitchen. It's this huge kitchen, she believes, with its French windows opening out into the courtyard garden, that makes the house the statement it is today.

'I didn't work with an architect,' Carina explains, 'as I love decorating and doing up houses myself.' One of her friends drew up her plans to scale, and a team of Polish builders and carpenters completed all of the work in just five months. Carina wanted to strike a balance between her own needs – to have a professional kitchen and a study to work from – and the importance of creating a home for her four girls. She decided to put the two youngest girls' bedrooms on the top floor, and to let the two teenagers live in the basement with their own private entrance. All of the living areas were designed to be at the centre of the house, and Carina's own bedroom is on the first floor, 'sandwiched in the middle'. To give the house continuity, she painted all of the rooms cream, while the doors and woodwork are pale blue.

When it came to designing the kitchen, Carina was inspired by the old dairies of France, with their cool marble counters, stainless-steel shelving and painted brick. Creating this space was a real labour of love: Carina found the perfect stainless-steel kitchen unit in Greece and had it shipped back, and re-created the look of an old storage larder when she brought back an old-fashioned fridge from Italy. Carina wanted to install work surfaces in dove-grey slate, but was unable to find the right colour. Instead, she simply picked up some shiny granite slabs and reversed them to create the perfect matte texture. Her two absolute essentials were a Wolf stainless-steel stove, 'which is like the Cadillac of cooking', and a working fireplace made from soft, cobbled brick. The new French windows initially overlooked a concrete yard, but Carina set to work to transform the space into a Mediterranean-inspired courtyard, with stone flooring, white-painted walls and a huge Moroccan mirror on one wall. When the sun comes out, the girls carry piles of cushions outside for impromptu lunches, using the space as it were an outdoor room.

For her own bedroom, bathroom and sitting room on the first floor, Carina wanted to re-create the understated feel of the French 1930s and 1940s. She chose neutral shades of beige and cream for the bedroom, with a folding suede screen that doubles up as a headboard behind the bed, and French zinc café tables from the 1930s, which are used for bedside tables. Because space was so limited, Carina placed her huge Arts and Crafts wardrobe out on the landing. The bathroom is decorated with different shades of pale grey marble to create an elegant hotel style, while across the hall in the sitting room, a French antique fireplace and 1940s mirror help to give the room an intimate feel. It is here that Carina has chosen to display photographs of her mother and grandmother, on a vintage Chinese table used specially to display favourite objects.

'If you have an aesthetic, it can spill over into every area of your life,' Carina remarks. 'I like to combine strange mixtures of fruit, vegetables and herbs that somehow go together, and my decorating is probably the same. It's a bit eclectic and one-offish.' She felt that her unusual Arts and Crafts house demanded a unique approach because of the quirky details, such as the central winding staircase leading to arched doorways and windows. This nineteenth-century house with its twenty-first-century extension somehow seems to fit this unconventional and creative family.

Wedgwood cabbage leaf plates are placed on top of a vintage tablecloth, laid over the kitchen table.

In the kitchen, Carina installed marble shelves and a vintage stainless-steel unit to suggest the feel of an old French dairy. The 1960s lamps, originally used in John Lewis, were picked up from salvage firm Lassco. 1940s French antiques provided the inspiration for the sitting room, and even the armchairs are covered in French linen. A vivid yellow vase from Sweden provides a shot of colour.

For her bedroom, Carina commissioned a suede screen that doubles up as a headboard and used French café tables from the 1930s to serve as elegant bedside tables. In one of her daughter's bedrooms, a trestle table has been transformed into a dressing table, accessorized with a vintage mirror, an antique chair and family photographs. A striped runner from **Roger Oates** adds bold colour to the oak staircase.

W11

NIKKI TIBBLES
NOTTING HILL

A riot of colour and a mix of hard-edged contemporary design with witty touches define this florist's home in a trendy, characterful neighbourhood.

Having trained as a florist, Nikki Tibbles loves to be surrounded by beautiful surroundings and greenery, so living in Notting Hill on a tree-lined street close to Hyde Park suits her perfectly. She shares her home with two rescue dogs, taking them for regular walks around the neighbourhood. Living in the super-trendy industrial neighbourhoods of the East End (like Whitechapel or Shoreditch) would be anathema to Nikki. As she explains, 'I like the beauty of the Victorian architecture around here and the lovely wide streets, which give you a real sense of space and sky.'

Despite her love of traditional architecture, Nikki chose to open her florist shop Wild at Heart on Turquoise Island in Westbourne Grove, a Postmodern pavilion designed by Piers Gough. Her contemporary designs have attracted a fashionable client list, and she numbers Chanel, Tiffany, Louis Vuitton and Betty Jackson among her patrons. When Wild and Heart first opened in 1993, it was surrounded by the hustle and bustle of Portobello Market, as well as antiques shops and galleries. But now many of the more quirky local stores have had to close. 'The area has changed a lot,' says Nikki. 'It doesn't have the colour and the diversity of people it used to, and some of the new shops are very high-street.' But Nikki still loves the neighbourhood and has lots of friends who live and work locally, including Tom Conran, the man behind Westbourne Grove favourite The Cow, and Sam Robinson, the co-owner of the influential boutique, The Cross (for Sam's own house, see p. 200).

Nikki moved into her Victorian house on a terraced Notting Hill street in 2001. 'The first thing I did when I moved in was to rip up the carpets, and paint the floorboards black and everything else white.' By 2006, she was tired of her white walls and repainted the whole house in 'Squirrel Grey' from Fired Earth, whose dense pigment reflects back the light. It also makes the perfect backdrop for her burgeoning art collection, which she has put together with the help of art dealer Max Wigram and art critic Tim Blanks. Two of the large photographs in the sitting room are from a series called 'Heart of Glass' by the fashion photographer Martyn Thompson.

Through her work at Wild at Heart, Nikki has built up a huge collection of contemporary and antique vases, which are displayed throughout the house. Favourite designs by Jonathan Adler and Nigel Coates can be seen in the sitting room, next to antique vases that Nikki picked up for a few pounds from Kempton Antiques Market. She has just started to collect Fulham vases in ice-cream shades, both glazed and unglazed, from the 1920s to the 1940s. Their organic shapes pick up on the feminine design of her bedroom, which has a deep grey bed from Edra, piled high with cushions in pink satin and black lace.

To make the house feel warm and inviting, Nikki turns on all of the lamps in every room when she gets home in the evening. Colour and texture are of primary importance, and Nikki enjoys playing with contrasts; the floral linen fabric by Bennison, for example, is an unexpected upholstery choice for a contemporary sofa in the sitting room. The curved lines of a black leather 'Egg' chair by Arne Jacobsen offset the bright prints of two Missoni cushions and an orange throw, while a huge striped painting by Anselm Reyle picks up on these bright colours and balances the graphic lines of a stainless-steel screen by Eileen Gray. In the kitchen and dining room, Nikki wanted to balance functional elements with more decorative touches, and to indulge for fondness for mixing antique and contemporary styles. She introduced wallpaper, pink velvet armchairs, oil paintings and vases to create a vintage feel in the dining room, while a huge white Anglepoise lamp provides a modern element. In the kitchen, an industrial-style stainless-steel cooker from Buyers and Sellers contrasts with an array of vintage paintings and a pink furry rug.

Living with two dogs, it is perhaps inevitable that they have started to take over the house, and their bright-pink sheepskin beanbags, together with an impressive collection of doggy artwork and sculptures, feature prominently. One recent acquisition is a charcoal sketch from the 1920s, which Nikki was drawn to because 'the dog's expression looks so human'. A collection that might have looked twee in any other house brings a much-needed dose of wit and humour to a stylish Notting Hill home.

A bouquet of old-fashioned roses from **Wild at Heart** was inspired by a favourite antique ceramic vase from **Kempton Antiques Market**.

The dining room's pink theme is enhanced by 1950s armchairs from Carden Cunietti and a rug by Tanya Thompson at Made. The oversized pink Anglepoise lamp is bespoke, and sits happily alongside a wooden table and benches from Kempton Antiques Market. In the kitchen, the hob is from Buyers and Sellers, the rug is from The Cross, and the vintage paintings were collected at antiques fairs.

The **L**-shaped sitting room is framed by **Michael Sodeau** wicker lamps and a **Terence Woodgate** sofa covered in linen from **Bennison**. The screen in front of the window is an **Eileen Gray** design, and the striped painting is by **Anselm Reyle**. The black leather chair is from **Themes & Variations**, while the fabric cushions are all from **Missoni**. In the dining room, the colour pink is a key design feature.

In front of the sofa is a pouf in textured wool from **Wild at Heart**. The Victorian buffet table against the wall holds **Veneti** vases by **Kenzo**, along with a paper sculpture by **Theresa Blackwell** made entirely from images of flowers cut from an illustrated book; above are two photographs from **Martyn Thompson's 'Heart of Glass'** series. In the hall landing, a papier-mâché dog keeps watch.

DIRECTORY

HOMEOWNERS

Norman Ackroyd
info@normanackroyd.com
www.normanackroyd.com

Bill Amberg
21–22 Chepstow Corner,
London W2 4XE
www.billamberg.com

Gillian Anderson-Price
Judith Michael & Daughter
73 Regent's Park Road,
London NW1 8UY
info@judithmichael.com
www.judithmichael.com

Harvey Bertram-Brown
renaissance_home@hotmail.com
www.thenewrenaissance.co.uk

Tracey Boyd
Tracey Boyd's House
42 Elizabeth Street,
London SW1W 9NZ
adrian@traceyboyd.com
www.traceyboyd.com

Emily Chalmers
Caravan
11 Lamb Street, London E1 6EA
info@caravanstyle.com
www.caravanstyle.com
emily@emilychalmers.com
www.emilychalmers.com

Jane Collins
Sixty6
66 Marylebone High Street,
London W1U 5JG

Rob + Josie da Bank
Bestival / Sunday Best
hello@bestival.net
www.bestival.net
info@sundaybest.net
www.sundaybest.net

Daisy de Villeneuve
daisy@daisydevilleneuve.com
www.daisydevilleneuve.com

Adam Hills + Maria Speake
Retrouvius
2A Ravensworth Road, London NW10 5NR
mail@retrouvius.com
www.retrouvius.com

Langlands + Bell
art@langlandsandbell.com
www.langlandsandbell.demon.co.uk

Annabel Lewis
V.V. Rouleaux
54 Sloane Square, London SW1W 8AX
sloane@vvrouleaux.com
102 Marylebone Lane, London W1U 2QD
marylebone@vvrouleaux.com
www.vvrouleaux.com

Victoria Marriott + Craig Matson
Roundhouse Design
25 Chalk Farm Road, London NW1 8AG
info@roundhousedesign.com
www.roundhousedesign.com

Peggy Prendeville
www.peggyprendeville.com

Sam Robinson
The Cross
141 Portland Road, London W11 4LW
Cross The Road
139 Portland Road, London W11 4LW

Tobit Roche
tobitroche@btinternet.com

Simon Templeton
mail@simontempleton.co.uk

Justin Thornton + Thea Bregazzi
Preen
5 Portobello Green,
281 Portobello Road, London W10 5TZ
sales@preen.eu
www.preen.eu

Nikki Tibbles
Wild at Heart
222 Westbourne Grove, London W11 2RJ
island@wildatheart.com
54 Pimlico Road, London SW1W 8LP
www.wildatheart.com

Les Trois Garçons
1 Club Row, London E1 6JX
www.lestroisgarcons.com

Lisa Whatmough
Squint
3 Redchurch Street,
London E2 7DJ
mail@squintlimited.com
www.squintlimited.com

Matthew Williamson
28 Bruton Street, London W1J 6QH
aitzi@matthewwilliamson.co.uk
www.matthewwilliamson.com

SUPPLIERS – PEOPLE

Jonathan Adler
web@jonathanadler.com
www.jonathanadler.com

Harry Allen
www.harryallendesign.com

Kate Blee
kate@kateblee.co.uk
www.kateblee.co.uk

Mark Brazier-Jones
studio@brazier-jones.com
www.brazier-jones.com

Rob + Nick Carter
rob@robandnick.com
www.robandnick.com

David Chipperfield
info@davidchipperfield.co.uk
www.davidchipperfield.co.uk

Nigel Coates
info@bransoncoates.com
www.nigelcoates.com

David Cobley
mail@davidcobley.co.uk
www.davidcobley.co.uk

Edmund de Waal
studio@edmunddewaal.com
www.edmunddewaal.com

Tom Dixon
sales@tomdixon.net
www.tomdixon.net

Rory Dobner
enquiries@rorydobner.com
www.rorydobner.com

Faile
info@faile.net
www.faile.net

Norman Foster
enquiries@fosterandpartners.com
www.fosterandpartners.com

Stefano Giovanonni
studio@stefanogiovannoni.it
www.stefanogiovannoni.it

Nick Helm
info@helmarchitecture.com
www.helmarchitecture.com

Sophie Herxheimer
sophie.herxheimer@talk21.com
www.sophieherxheimer.com

Nicholas Hills
info@nicholas-hills-architects.co.uk
www.nicholas-hills-architects.co.uk

Suzy Hoodless
info@suzyhoodless.com
www.suzyhoodless.com

Arne Jacobsen
www.arne-jacobsen.com

Chris Kenny
info@englandgallery.com
www.englandgallery.com

Gerald Laing
www.geraldlaing.com

Fliff Lidsey
www.fliff.co.uk

Ian McKeever
www.ianmckeever.com

Shirley McLauchlan
www.skmclauchlan.co.uk

Verner Panton
www.vernerpanton.com

Ernest Race
enquiries@racefurniture.com
www.racefurniture.com

Rodnik
sales@rodnik.co.uk
www.rodnik.co.uk

Peter Saville
www.saville-associates.com

Nigel Shafran
www.nigelshafran.com

Michael Sodeau
info@michaelsodeau.com
www.michaelsodeau.com

Rupert Spira
www.rupertspira.com

Philippe Starck
www.philippe-starck.com

Martyn Thompson
info@martynthompson.com
www.martynthompsonstudio.com

Georgiana von Etzdorf
www.gvc.co.uk

Miv Watts
mivwatts@btconnect.com
www.wattswishedfor.co.uk

SUPPLIERS – PLACES

Absolute Flowers
14 Clifton Road, London W9 1SS
flowers@absoluteflowersandhome.com
www. absoluteflowersandhome.com

Alfies Antique Market
13–25 Church Street,
London NW8 8DT
info@alfiesantiques.com
www.alfiesantiques.com

Anthropologie
worldservice@anthropologie.com
www.anthropologie.com

Aria
Barnsbury Hall
Barnsbury Street,
London N1 1PN
design@ariashop.co.uk
www.aria-shop.co.uk

B&B Italia
250 Brompton Road,
London SW3 2AS
store.london@bebitalia.it
www.london.bebitalia.com

Bathstore
info@bathstore.com
www.bathstore.com

Bazar Antiques
82 Golborne Road,
London W10 5PS

Bennison Fabrics
6 Holbein Place, London SW1W 8NL
bennisonfabrics@btinternet.com
www.bennisonfabrics.com

Biba
info@bibaexperience.com
www.bibaexperience.com

Boffi Chelsea
250 Brompton Road,
London SW3 2AS
info@boffichelsea.com
www.boffi.com

Boom Interiors
115–117 Regents Park Road,
London NW1 8UR
info@boominteriors.com
www.boominteriors.com

Browns Focus
38–39 South Molton Street,
London W1K 5RN
brownsfocus@brownsfashion.com
www.brownsfashion.com

Butcher Plasterworks
Chalcot Yard, 8 Fitzroy Road,
London NW1 8TX
post@butcherplasterworks.com
www.butcherplasterworks.com

Buyers and Sellers
Unit 8, Royalty Studios
105–109 Lancaster Road,
London W11 1QF
sales@buyersandsellersonline.co.uk
www.buyersandsellersonline.co.uk

By Guru
info@by-guru.com
www.by-guru.com

Cappellini
www.cappellini.it

Carden Cunietti
1a Adpar Street, London W2 1DE
cc@carden-cunietti.com
www.carden-cunietti.com

Castle Gibson
106a Upper Street,
London N1 1QN
www.castlegibson.com

Cath Kidston
www.cathkidston.co.uk

Celia Birtwell
71 Westbourne Park Road,
London W2 5QH
info@celiabirtwell.com
www.celiabirtwell.com

Chaplins
sales@chaplins.co.uk
www.chaplins.co.uk

Cole & Son
Chelsea Harbour Design Centre
Lots Road, London SW10 0XE
customer.service@cole-and-son.com
www.cole-and-son.com

Colefax & Fowler
110 Fulham Road,
London SW3 6HU
www.colefax.com

The Conran Shop
Michelin House
81 Fulham Road,
London SW3 6RD
www.conranshop.co.uk

Dalsouple
info@dalsouple.com
www.dalsouple.com

Designers Guild
267 & 277 King's Road,
London SW3 5EN
showroom@designersguild.com
www.designersguild.com

Dosa
mail@dosainc.com
www.dosainc.com

Dover Street Market
17–18 Dover Street, London W1S 4LT
info@doverstreetmarket.com
www.doverstreetmarket.com

Edra
edra@edra.com
www.edra.com

Fandango
50 Cross Street,
London N1 2BA

Farrow & Ball
info@farrow-ball.com
www.farrow-ball.com

Felix Spicer Fabrics
141 Pancras Road,
London NW1 1UN
felixspicer@felixspicer.co.uk
www.felixspicer.co.uk

Fired Earth
enquiries@firedearth.com
www.firedearth.com

George Smith Hand-Made
Furniture and Fabrics
www.georgesmith.com

Ghost
36 Ledbury Road,
London W11 2AB
info@ghost.co.uk
www.ghost.co.uk

Glass Deco
info@glass-deco.com
www.glass-deco.com

Globe-Trotter
54–55 Burlington Arcade, London W1J 0LB
info@globemack.co.uk
www.globe-trotterltd.com

Habitat
www.habitat.co.uk

Harvey Nichols
109–125 Knightsbridge, London SW1X 7RJ
contactknightsbridge@harveynichols.com
www.harveynichols.com

Heal's
enquiries@heals.co.uk
www.heals.co.uk

Holmegaard
www.holmegaard.com

House of Baguettes
info@houseofbaguette.com
www.houseofbaguette.com

Ikea
www.ikea.com

Intertiles
102 Balls Pond Road, London N1 4AG
www.inter-tiles.co.uk

Joss Graham
10 Eccleston Street, London SW1W 9LT
www.jossgraham.com

John Lewis
Oxford Street, London W1A 1EX
www.johnlewis.com

Judy Greenwood Antiques
657–659 Fulham Road,
London SW6 5PY

Kempton Antiques Market
enquiries@kemptonantiques.co.uk
www.kemptonantiques.com

Lassco
Brunswick House
30 Wandsworth Road, London SW8 2LG
brunswick@lassco.co.uk
www.lassco.co.uk

Laura Ashley
www.lauraashley.com

Liberty
Regent Street, London W1B 5AH
londonstorecustomerservices@liberty.co.uk
www.liberty.co.uk

Made
21a Silchester Road, London W10 6SF
info@made.co.uk
www.made.co.uk

La Maison
107–108 Shoreditch High Street,
London E1 6JN
info@atlamaison.com
www.atlamaison.com

Maisonette
9 Chamberlayne Road,
London NW10 3ND

Marimekko
www.marimekko.com

Martin Margiela
presse@martinmargiela.net
www.maisonmartinmargiela.com

Megan Park
65 Leonard Street,
London EC2A 4QS
neil@meganpark.co.uk
www.meganpark.co.uk

Mint
79 Wigmore Street, London W1U 2SF
info@mintshop.co.uk
www.mintshop.co.uk

Missoni
www.missonihome.com

Myriad Antiques
131 Portland Road,
London, W11 4LW

Neisha Crosland
8 Elystan Street, London SW3 3NS
elystanstreet@neishacrosland.com
www.neishacrosland.com

Osborne & Little
304 King's Road, London SW3 5UH
www.osborneandlittle.com

Petersham Nurseries
info@petershamnurseries.com
www.petershamnurseries.com

Portobello Road Market
info@portobelloroad.co.uk
www.portobelloroad.co.uk

Pucci
www.emiliopucci.com

Rainbow
329 Lillie Road,
London SW6 7NR
info@rainbowlondon.com
www.rainbowlondon.com

Ralph Lauren
www.ralphlauren.com

Roger Oates
1 Munro Terrace,
London SW10 0DL
www.rogeroates.com

The Rug Company
124 Holland Park Avenue,
London W11 4UE
london@therugcompany.info
www.therugcompany.info

Savoir Beds
104 Wigmore Street,
London W1U 3RN
info@savoirbeds.co.uk
www.savoirbeds.co.uk

Sheila Cook Textiles
105–107 Portobello Road,
London W11 1QB
sheilacook@sheilacook.co.uk
www.sheilacook.co.uk

Shiu-Kay Kan
skk@easynet.co.uk
www.skk.net

Space Boudoir
214 Westbourne Grove,
London W11 2RH

Squires Antiques
squiresantiques@aol.com
www.squiresantiques.com

Tann-Rokka
123 Regents Park Road,
London NW1 8BE
info@tannrokka.com
www.tannrokka.com

Themes & Variations
231 Westbourne Grove,
London W11 2SE
go@themesandvariations.com
www.themesandvariations.com

Tile & Stone Magic
info@tilemagic.co.uk
www.tilemagic.co.uk

Timorous Beasties
46 Amwell Street,
London EC1R 1XS
london@timorousbeasties.com
www.timorousbeasties.com

TopShop
36–38 Great Castle Street,
London W1W 8LG
www.topshop.com

Tuchra
82 Wandsworth Bridge Road,
London SW6 2TF

Vivienne Westwood
info@viviennewestwood.co.uk
www.viviennewestwoodonline.co.uk

Wolf Appliance
www.wolfappliance.com

Zoffany
Chelsea Harbour Design Centre
Lots Road, London SW10 0XE
enquiries@zoffany.uk.com
www.zoffany.com